War Games

Linda Polman is the author of *We Did Nothing: Why the Truth Doesn't Always Come Out When the UN Goes In*, which was shortlisted for the Lettre Ulysses and the Index on Censorship awards. She studied at the School of Journalism in Utrecht and for the past twenty years has been a freelance journalist for international radio, TV and newspapers; she is a contributor to *The Times* and the *Guardian*. After *We Did Nothing* she lived and worked as a correspondent in Sierra Leone and Liberia for several years. She currently resides in Holland, where she is a guest lecturer for the School of Journalism, for Dutch military academies and for several faculties for International Relationships and International Development Cooperation Studies in Dutch universities.

Liz Waters has translated a wide range of quality non-fiction books from Dutch into English. She lives in Amsterdam.

War Games

The Story of Aid and War in Modern Times

LINDA POLMAN

Translated by Liz Waters

VIKING

an imprint of

PENGUIN BOOKS

Published by the Penguin Group
Penguin Books Ltd, 80 Strand, London WC2R ORL, England
Penguin Group (USA) Inc., 375 Hudson Street, New York, New York 10014, USA
Penguin Group (Canada), 90 Eglinton Avenue East, Suite 700, Toronto, Ontario, Canada M4P 2Y3
(a division of Pearson Penguin Canada Inc.)
Penguin Ireland, 25 St Stephen's Green, Dublin 2, Ireland (a division of Penguin Books Ltd)
Penguin Group (Australia), 250 Camberwell Road, Camberwell, Victoria 3124, Australia
(a division of Pearson Australia Group Pty Ltd)
Penguin Books India Pvt Ltd, 11 Community Centre, Panchsheel Park, New Delhi – 110017, India
Penguin Group (NZ), 67 Apollo Drive, Rosedale, North Shore 0632, New Zealand
(a division of Pearson New Zealand Ltd)
Penguin Books (South Africa) (Pty) Ltd, 24 Sturdee Avenue, Rosebank, Johannesburg 2196, South Africa

Penguin Books Ltd, Registered Offices: 80 Strand, London WC2R ORL, England

www.penguin.com

First published 2010

3

Set in Bembo Book MT Std 12/14.75pt
Typeset by Ellipsis Books Limited, Glasgow
Printed in Great Britain by Clays Ltd, St Ives plc

A CIP catalogue record for this book is available from the British Library

ISBN: 978-0-670-91896-6

www.greenpenguin.co.uk

Contents

Preface:
Imagine. You get a phone call . . .

The humane desire to lighten a little the torments of all these poor
wretches [. . .] creates a kind of energy which gives one a positive
craving to relieve as many as one can.

Henri Dunant, humanitarian aid worker and founder of the
International Committee of the Red Cross[1]

Imagine. You're an international humanitarian aid worker in a
war zone and faithful to the principles of the Red Cross, as any
good humanitarian should be. In other words, you're impartial,
neutral and independent. It's your responsibility to relieve human
suffering, irrespective of the people involved and the situation on
the ground.

This time your mission has taken you to a refugee camp in Darfur.
You do what you can for the victims, but soldiers exploit your
efforts. They demand money for every well you dig and levy
sky-high taxes, thought up on the spot, on all the sacks of rice and
tents and medicines you arrange to have flown in. They consume a
slice of your aid supplies and sell another slice. Among the items
they buy with the proceeds are weapons, which they use to drive
yet more people into your refugee camp or even to their deaths.

What do you do?

A. Despite an extremely difficult situation, you preserve your
neutrality and do what you can for the victims.
B. You evaluate the circumstances, conclude that the principles
of the Red Cross can no longer be applied here, and leave.

Imagine. You belong to the local regime and you busy yourself
finding ways of using relief funds, intended for the refugee camp,

to your own advantage. Then on the shimmering horizon you see a dust cloud moving towards you. Inside is a convoy of white Land Cruisers. They stop at the gates to the camp. Windows slide open and politicians from Washington, New York and London stick their heads out. They loftily inform you that their financing of the international aid effort in the camp will be dependent in future on your determination and practical steps to put an end to the violence in the region and the theft of aid supplies. Then they wind up their windows and the procession lurches off towards the horizon.

What do you do?

A. You tackle the violence and stop stealing.
B. You let them sound off. Without money from donor governments the refugees will starve to death and there's no way the donors are going to allow that.

Now you're the humanitarian aid worker again. You've been listening in on the conversation. Before the parade of representatives of donor governments is even out of sight, the looting of aid supplies resumes and soldiers drive more refugees into the camp at gunpoint.

What do you do?

A. It's completely impossible to cling to the principles of the Red Cross any longer. You ring Washington, New York and London to tell them they must cut off the flow of money. Then you pack your bags and leave to help war victims elsewhere.
B. Even if you save only one human life, some relief is better than none. So you remain true to your principles and ring your contractor to order foodstuffs and medicines to replace the stolen supplies. You ask him to make a speedy delivery, since every day brings yet more refugees for you to feed.

Leave, or continue providing aid at any price? It's a centuries-old dilemma. Two of the world's first international humanitarian aid workers, Florence Nightingale and Henri Dunant, fundamentally disagreed as to which would be the right choice. Nightingale was convinced that aid fails in its purpose if the warring parties use it to their own advantage; Dunant firmly believed in the duty to help no matter what.

Henri Dunant, born into a Calvinistic milieu in Switzerland, was a banker and businessman in Geneva. In 1859 he witnessed the Battle of Solferino during the war between Austria and the Franco-Sardinian Alliance. Of the 300,000 men and boys on the front line in Lombardy, 40,000 were killed. Another 40,000 soldiers were wounded. They lay on the battlefield, where most were left to die.

In the book that Dunant published three years after this experience, *Un Souvenir de Solferino* (*A Memory of Solferino*), he describes the spectacle the morning after the engagement:

Bodies of men and horses covered the battlefield; corpses were strewn over roads, ditches, ravines, thickets and fields; the approaches to Solferino were literally thick with dead. The poor wounded men were ghostly pale and exhausted. [. . .] Some, who had gaping wounds already beginning to show infection, were almost crazed with suffering. They begged to be put out of their misery, and writhed with faces distorted in the grip of the death struggle. [. . .] In some quarters there was no water, and the thirst was so terrible that officers and men alike fell to drinking from muddy pools whose water was foul and filled with curdled blood. The men's wounds were covered with flies. The tunic, shirt, flesh and blood formed an indescribable mass, alive with vermin.

Wounded Austrian soldiers told Dunant that after a long, sweltering march they had been sent straight into battle, without a chance to rest and without being given anything to eat or drink, save a brandy ration. French soldiers too had marched for days on end to reach the front. On the morning of the battle they'd had nothing besides a mug of coffee.

For lack of sufficient army doctors, it was the inhabitants of the villages and small towns in the vicinity of Solferino who set about helping the wounded, with bandages and water. The volunteers carried surviving soldiers to stables, churches and monasteries, where they helped a handful of village doctors to amputate limbs. In the circumstances little other medical help could be given.

'The convoys brought a fresh contingent of wounded men [. . .] every quarter of an hour, and the shortage of assistants, orderlies and helpers was cruelly felt,' wrote Dunant. He gathered together a group of volunteers, mainly women.

Nearly five hundred soldiers were there, piled in the church, and a hundred more lay outside on straw in front of the church, with strips of canvas to protect them from the sun. The women [. . .] went from one man to another with jars and canteens full of pure water to quench their thirst and moisten their wounds.

Dunant arranged for cauldrons of soup to be prepared and he supplied the volunteers with large bales of lint for cleaning wounds. From a town some distance away he had medicines, shirts, oranges and tobacco brought in at his own expense.

'*Tutti fratelli*,' was Dunant's conviction, we are all brothers. He successfully persuaded the volunteers to help all wounded men, Austrians included. In the days that followed, 'noble philanthropists' and 'ladies' auxiliary committees' established for the occasion each made it a point of honour to care for wounded soldiers, irrespective of nationality.

Every house for kilometres around was turned into a clinic. People doled out soup, wrote farewell letters to families on behalf of dying soldiers and patted blood-encrusted hands comfortingly. They meant well, Dunant wrote, but the volunteers were and remained 'isolated enthusiasts' making 'dispersed efforts'. The food delivered by injudicious townspeople to the churches and hospitals was often unsuitable for wounded men and eventually the doors had to be shut to them.

The consequence was that many, who would have been willing to spend an hour or two with the patients, would not be bothered when it became necessary to have an authorization and go and ask for it. [. . .] There was no time for those who knew their business to give the needful advice and guidance, and most of those who brought their own goodwill to the task lacked the necessary knowledge and experience, so that their efforts were inadequate and often ineffective.

Although they had started out in real earnest, within a week the enthusiasm of the volunteers began to ebb. They became exhausted.

'Oh,' sighed Dunant, 'how valuable it would have been in those Lombardy towns to have had a hundred experienced and qualified voluntary orderlies and nurses! Such a group would have formed a nucleus around which could have been rallied the scanty help and dispersed efforts which needed competent guidance.'

Back in Switzerland he lobbied for just such a private initiative. In a proposal sent to potential donors he argued that the work of the new organization would not only be humane and Christian, it would benefit the national treasury. 'By reducing the number of cripples, a saving would be effected in the expenses of a Government which has to provide pensions for disabled soldiers,' he wrote.

This last point was precisely the reason why the other great humanitarian of the period, the British nurse Florence Nightingale, rejected Dunant's plan out of hand. The higher the costs of a war, the sooner it would end, she argued. Voluntary efforts, which reduced the expense faced by war ministries, merely made it easier for governments to engage in wars more often and for longer.

In 1854, five years before Dunant's experiences at the Battle of Solferino, Nightingale, then thirty-four, had responded to a request from the War Office to assist the sick and wounded British troops of the Crimean War. The War Office was under fire in the British press over the inadequate care being given to the men.

Along with a team of thirty-eight professional nurses, whom she selected herself, Nightingale travelled to the British barracks at

Scutari in Istanbul, on the Asian shore of the Bosporus. Stinking wards with leaking roofs, filled to bursting, were all that was available in the way of an army hospital there. Unwashed soldiers still wearing their soiled uniforms lay dying in agony in beds without sheets or blankets. There were not enough medicines, bandages, soap or food. The medical staff refused to order further supplies, afraid that commanding officers would take it as personal criticism.

'Patients were left in the care of drunken orderlies who were often malingering soldiers, thieves avid for the savings of the dying, or pensioners who had foolishly volunteered to come out of retirement to accompany the army and who were rapidly succumbing to disease and delirium tremens,' writes British author Hugh Small in his book *Florence Nightingale: Avenging Angel*.[2]

Conditions at other British military hospitals in the East were similarly abominable. The Crimean War lasted from October 1853 to February 1856. A total of 18,000 men died, out of an army theoretically 25,000 strong. Five out of every six deaths were caused by cholera, dysentery, typhus and other infections.

Dead animals littered the site of Nightingale's hospital, the yards outside the buildings were unpaved and poorly drained, and water stood stagnant in the sewers running under the unventilated buildings. Only after a visit from a Sanitary Commission sent from London were the medical staff ordered, at the commission's insistence, to reduce the double rows of beds in each corridor to a single row, and to have orderlies empty the rubbish bins and urine containers.

The death rate was highest in wards where the consequences of poor hygiene were exacerbated by overcrowding. The most deadly place of all, where 5,000 men succumbed in a single winter, was Nightingale's own hospital. She was managing not a hospital but a death camp. In letters home she placed the responsibility for this wholesale 'killing' on British officers of the 'incompetent and heartless' Army High Command who were, in her words, 'sordid exploiters of human misery'.

The dedication with which her team of nurses attempted to look after the men as they lay dying distracted attention from the causes of the disaster, Nightingale concluded later. The only way to save lives was to make costly investments in better hygiene and buildings. Civil servants at the War Office removed the most damaging passages from her report before it was presented to parliament. The war was not yet over and Nightingale's charts, which laid bare the causes of sickness and death, would have made it even harder for the War Office to enlist new recruits and mercenaries.

Nightingale devoted the rest of her life to nominating and keeping on their toes the only people who could improve conditions for soldiers, and later for ordinary citizens as well: the legislative and executive authorities. When Henri Dunant in Switzerland began to lobby for an international volunteer organization to help wounded soldiers, and by doing so relieve the government of its responsibilities, Nightingale felt only anger and disgust. Dunant wrote to try to convince her that his initiative was crucial. He agreed that war ministries bore primary responsibility for the care of their own sick and wounded, but even in the best organized armies such care was inadequate. Nightingale answered tartly: 'If the present Regulations are not sufficient to provide for the wounded they should be made so.'

Although Dunant was a self-declared admirer of 'Miss Nightingale', her disapproval left him undaunted. In 1863, nine years after the Crimean War and four years after Solferino, Dunant and other Genevan notables set up the International Committee of the Red Cross (ICRC), the forerunner of all Western humanitarian aid organizations in existence today. The 'humanitarian' principles adopted by the ICRC became entrenched in the Geneva Conventions.

Humanitarianism is based on a presumed duty to ease human suffering unconditionally. Aid organizations endorsing the humanitarian principles of the Red Cross promise neutrality (no cooperation with one side in preference to the other), impartiality (the giving of aid purely according to need) and independence (from geopolitical, military or other interests). Humanitarian aid workers help wherever, whenever and whomever they can. *Tutti fratelli.*

'I need hardly say that I think its views most absurd,' Nightingale continued to complain, 'just such as would originate in a little state like Geneva, which never can see war.'

Signatures by Nauru and Montenegro in August 2006 mean that the Geneva Conventions have now been accepted by all 194 countries in the world. Never before have the principles of the Red Cross been so universally embraced. And never have there been so many humanitarian aid organizations. They are known as NGOs, Non-Governmental Organizations, or INGOs if they work internationally: independent and neutral organizations not tied to governments. Together they make up the 'humanitarian community' that operates in 'humanitarian territories', places conceived as enclaves in war zones where the provision of aid to victims transcends all military and political imperatives. Victims are victims, irrespective of cause and effect.

In the century and a half that has passed since the ICRC was established, its principles have remained the same while wars and humanitarian territories have changed utterly. In Dunant's time wars were still fought on battlefields, and almost all the dead and wounded were soldiers. A hundred years later, after the Second World War, the decision was made to declare Red Cross principles applicable to aid offered to civilians in wartime. Civilians had become military targets, bombed in their cities and towns, persecuted, and the target of extermination programmes. The Second World War claimed roughly equal numbers of military and civilian victims. In our own time as many as 90 per cent of war fatalities are civilians and almost all wars are civil wars, fought not by the armies of belligerent nations but by people's militias, separatist movements, insurgents and rebels within the war-torn country itself. A government army, if involved at all, is merely one of the parties to a conflict, of which there are usually several.

Today's humanitarian territories, in which the humanitarian community attempts to reduce human suffering, are to be found in countries such as Iraq and Afghanistan, where the fighting is messy and long drawn out, and in Congo, Somalia, Sierra Leone, Ethiopia and Sudan, hellish places where one of the main goals of the warring factions is to slaughter as many civilians as possible and drive all the survivors out of house and home. Humanitarian territories and battlefields are often one and the same, since civilians gather there, clustered around the aid organizations.

Humanitarian aid workers still help wherever, whenever and whomever they can, as a matter of principle, but by doing so they are at the mercy of the belligerents and become subject to their whims. The tragedy of the admirable Red Cross rules is that they are unenforceable. 'In this kind of war, calling on, or expecting, the parties to respect humanitarian principles is like calling on a gang of armed muggers to fight by the rules of boxing; it's not just laughable, it's irrelevant,' said a victim of the Afghan war.[3]

Should INGOs carry on doggedly providing relief if warring factions in humanitarian territories both use aid for their own benefit, to the detriment of their enemies, and prolong the fighting? Or should they leave? Which option, in the long run, is more cruel?

The dilemma faced by Dunant and Nightingale is more pressing than ever.

After the Second World War, during the Cold War, conflict zones were more or less inaccessible to private humanitarian aid organizations. The world was divided into East and West, and the boundaries of war-torn areas were controlled by the two superpowers. INGOs did not usually get any closer to the seats of conflict than refugee camps on the peripheries of war zones.

Around 1989 and the fall of the Berlin Wall, the nature of armed conflict changed and with it the position of aid organizations. In many areas the superpowers withdrew. From then on it was the local warring parties themselves who decided when and on what conditions organizations would be given access to victims. The number of aid agencies in war zones has since vastly increased. In the 1980s 'only' around forty INGOs were active in the camps set up for Cambodian refugees near the border with Thailand. Fifteen years later, in 1994–5, 250 came to the war in former Yugoslavia. Favoured humanitarian territories can now bank on the arrival not only of INGOs but of an average of ten different UN relief agencies and literally countless local NGOs. The ICRC reckons that every major disaster now attracts, again on average, about 1,000 national and international aid organizations. The presence of twice that number, as in Afghanistan in 2004, no longer surprises anyone. The United Nations Development Programme (UNDP) estimates that the total number of international NGOs exceeds 37,000.

For developmental cooperation in general, donor governments that belong to the Organisation for Economic Co-operation and Development (OECD) make a total of about $120 billion available annually. For emergency humanitarian relief – first-aid, you might say, for wars and disasters – the sum reached $11.2 billion in 2008, not including incidental extras, for use in case of an event such as a tsunami, or for emergency assistance given by soldiers in front-line states in the War on Terror. Campaigns by churches, businesses and clubs, plus door-to-door collections and all kinds of spontaneous, heart-warming local initiatives, add hundreds of millions of dollars to this total every year. An entire industry has grown up around humanitarian aid, with cavalcades of organizations following the flow of money and competing with each other in one humanitarian territory after another for the biggest achievable share of the billions.

To warring parties as well, money and supplies provided by humanitarian aid organizations represent a business opportunity. Aid has become a permanent feature of military strategy. Belligerents see to it that the enemy is given as little as possible while they themselves get hold of as much as they can.

No matter how often the Red Cross rules may be trampled underfoot by warlords, generals, rebel leaders, agitators, local chiefs, insurgents, heads of splinter-groups, militia commanders, transnational terrorist leaders, regime bosses, mercenaries, freedom fighters and national and international governments, the humanitarians persist in brandishing their Red Cross principles and accept no responsibility for the abuse of their aid.

Ranging from the huge, well-oiled humanitarian operations run by the ICRC in the sandy deserts and rocky wastes of the Horn of Africa or by the UN refugee organization UNHCR beyond the Sahara to a one-man aid mission on a backfiring moped in Rwanda, and from the rapid front-line interventions by Oxfam in the craggy mountains of Afghanistan or by Médecins sans Frontières (MSF) in Ethiopia to the floating clinics of the Mercy Ships from Texas that drop anchor on the shores of West African civil wars in the name of the Redeemer, a caravanserai of humanitarian aid organizations treks, apparently by common agreement, from one humanitarian territory to the next. In this book we travel with them, through overcrowded, stinking refugee camps, via food distribution points in famine zones to bombed and shelled villages and towns, and to homes for war orphans.

One question inevitably arises. If aid has become a strategic aspect of warfare, can the claim to neutrality made by humanitarian aid organizations still be justified? Reduced to a single horrific episode in our own history, this dilemma becomes easier to comprehend.

Imagine. It's 1943. You're an international aid worker. The telephone rings. It's the Nazis. You'll be granted permission to deliver aid to the concentration camps, but the camp management will decide how much of it goes to its own staff and how much to the prisoners.

What do you do?

If you conform to the practices of the humanitarian aid industry, you'll deliver the supplies.

1. Goma: a 'total ethical disaster'

April 1995. From the battered road barrier on the Rwandan side of the border to the open plain crowded with refugees on the Zairean side was a walk of perhaps a kilometre. Above my negotiations with the Zairean border guards I could already hear the sound made by three-quarters of a million camp-dwellers. A threatening hum, as if a giant wasps' nest awaited me.

I'd covered 300 metres, through muddy puddles and past deep ruts in the road, when a man on a bicycle slowed down to ride next to me at walking pace.

'Taxi?' the cyclist asked.

'Nuh, I'm just about there now,' I answered.

'Aha, so you know where they are today?' The man, an African, spoke French.

'Where what are?' I asked him.

'*Bon*, so you don't.' He was wearing a tattered jacket and pedalling with bare feet. 'The mines. You don't know where they are today. Every night we put them in different puddles or cracks in the tarmac. Only yesterday a white woman from the American Refugee Committee found one. Boom! Both legs blown off. You'd better ride with me. I'm Hutu; I help lay the mines. *Montez, s'il vous plaît.*' He pointed invitingly to his baggage rack.

At first it was all downhill. Over his shoulder he chattered away nineteen to the dozen about the international aid agencies that were helping the Hutus in the camps. Lately most humanitarians hadn't started work till after lunch, he told me. 'They wait for someone else to test the road in a car. Everyone who drives along here after that sticks to the tyre tracks of the first vehicle of the day. Or maybe they'll send their African drivers ahead of them before setting out themselves. *Les salauds!*'

With a tug at the handlebars he swerved to avoid a group of local men who were filling a large pot-hole with some of the chunks of lava that lay scattered everywhere at the side of the road.

He pointed: 'The American's hole.'

The mining of the road by the Hutus in the camps was part of a military strategy, he explained. 'The hidden explosives are there to make sure the cockroaches don't dare come and attack us.' By cockroaches he meant the Rwandan Tutsis, compatriots of his but from a different ethnic group. The mines also served to persuade any Hutus considering going back to Rwanda to think twice or three times about it. 'Not that there are many of those, mind you, traitors who want to go and live with the cockroaches again,' he assured me.

The road was slightly uphill now, and busier. Apparently there was less danger of explosions this close to the camp. First hundreds, then thousands, then tens of thousands of Hutus swarmed along and across the tarmac. Endless lines were making their way on foot to the forested volcanic slopes up ahead to gather firewood, and groups composed mainly of women called out in high-pitched voices as they walked along the verge with mattresses and baskets brimming with vegetables on their heads, all of it for sale. We weaved between children wheeling bicycles and hand-carts stacked high with tarpaulins and sacks of charcoal, and forced our way, braking and accelerating by turns, through a congested mass of dented vans and old taxis. Tilting under their loads of people and luggage, the vehicles were heading for the town of Goma a few kilometres away. A fleet of white Land Cruisers belonging to international aid workers navigated a passage between the tooting and honking Hutus. My chauffeur didn't take his hand off his bicycle bell for a second; our approach sounded like the coming of the ice-cream man.

'Busy here,' I remarked to the toiling back in front of me. Like Fred Flintstone, my feet thrusting against the ground, I helped move the bicycle forwards.

'You should have seen it here last year,' my driver gasped. 'We all came along this road at the same time, out of Rwanda. There were blockages everywhere, caused by people falling down dead. Of cholera, mostly.'

Our front wheel knocked against the bumper of a Land Cruiser belonging to the International Red Cross.

The electronically operated window on the driver's side instantly whirred open.

A white face emerged. 'Watch where you're going, *imbécile*!' it shouted.

'Watch out yourself! Pig!' my lift screamed back, but the window had already hummed shut. 'Your mother's a whore!' he shouted, but to me he said, friendliness personified, '*Voilà*, Camp Mugunga. Here you'll always find white brothers and sisters. That'll be ten dollars, please.'

For the sake of the ensuing ritual I looked as tight-fisted as I could.

'One,' I said firmly. We settled on $3 plus a roll of film. I pulled a HEMA home-brand roll out of my bag.

'Aha!' the cyclist went, pleased. 'I know that brand. It's very good!'

He said good day and wormed his way back into the stream of traffic, ringing his bell. While a Hercules transport plane full of aid supplies descended low over my head, bound for the landing strip further on, I stepped across a rubbish-clogged ditch. I was entering the largest of Goma's twenty-five refugee camps.

Mother Africa sure has given birth to some poisonous snakes, the Africans say. The Great Lakes Region between Rwanda and the Democratic Republic of Congo (in those days still called Zaire) is one of them. Every single ingredient of war on the African continent is present here, combined in a dreadful mix: monstrous poverty, underpaid government soldiers and drug-fuelled militias, easily recruited gangs of futureless youngsters, new political leaders and the still militant supporters of old chiefs, interference by neighbouring African states and by non-African countries, unstable political, social, economic and cultural relationships, perpetually shifting coalitions, an illegal trade in coffee, diamonds, oil and cheap weapons (everything from machetes to second-hand fighter planes), mercenaries, refugees and the displaced.

When on 6 April 1994 the genocide by extremist Rwandan Hutus of their Tutsi fellow citizens began, few people outside Rwanda had any idea of the deep, dark currents that were disturbing local politics. Far from everyone in Rwanda knew all the ins and outs either; if they had, more Tutsis would have fled in time. Initially the outside world saw only what bubbled to the surface of that infernal witches' brew. First came the mutilated corpses floating day and night down the rivers that flow out of Rwanda's 'thousand hills' into the Great Lakes. In the space of three weeks, 800,000 Rwandan Tutsis and moderate Hutus were slaughtered by their extremist Hutu compatriots. Next the international camera teams that had rushed to the region filmed a mass of humanity descending out of Rwanda towards the lakes. In just a few weeks an estimated 2 million Rwandans managed to cross the southern and south-eastern borders, in trucks, in private cars or on bicycles and mopeds, pushing wheelbarrows, running, stumbling, pursued by a Tutsi army that had invaded from Uganda to the north and put an end to the genocide.

Most television viewers in the West had only just woken up to the fact that an attempt to exterminate an entire people had taken place in Rwanda. The refugees they saw on the news, trudging out of the country, were clearly fleeing from something horrific. Television viewers assumed these were the survivors of the slaughter. In fact they were the perpetrators of the genocide. The stream of refugees included the entire Rwandan Hutu army and tens of thousands of members of extremist citizens' militias that had helped carry out the killings in Rwanda. The few roads in the border area were soon utterly congested. The flight of the Hutus was the biggest, fastest and least understood exodus in the history of humanitarian relief.

Several hundred thousand Hutus descended on neighbouring Tanzania and Burundi, but the stream of refugees that sucked up by far the most media attention was the one that poured across the barren plain below the Nyarangongo volcano near Goma in former Zaire, close to the barriers that marked the border with Rwanda. Three-quarters of a million strong, it was the largest of the three, and it was the only one that could be watched live on television. Goma's landing strip, around which the refugees gathered, was long enough for the huge transport aircraft in which, along with the first shipments of aid supplies, international aid agencies ferried journalists to the scene. International camera teams needed only to walk down the aircraft steps to be able to send images around the world by satellite of a great mass of humanity, exhausted and hungry after the long trek out of Rwanda. Goma would go down in the annals of humanitarian aid as, among other things, 'the crisis with the landing strip effect'.

In the early weeks it seemed as if just as many media organizations as aid agencies had swooped down upon the Hutu refugees. Around 500 journalists, cameramen and sound technicians were stumbling about on a patch of land some fifty kilometres long and one kilometre wide. Most journalists presented the story in heart-rending terms as a humanitarian drama. Either they failed to understand the political context or they ignored it. The same went for their main informants, Western aid workers. Most were young and inexperienced, since organizations had been forced to recruit new staff as rapidly as possible. For many, Goma was their first foreign aid mission.

In pouring rain, under banana leaves and bits of cardboard, the refugees waited in Goma's parks, streets, alleyways, churches and schools, and on roadside verges, for someone to do something for them. When cholera broke out in the desolate, sodden sea of humanity, the scenes were ghastly. The dying began. Six hundred deaths from cholera a day quickly grew to an estimated daily toll of 3,000. The disease killed a total of perhaps 50,000 Hutus, the elderly and children first. Some journalists called it a 'second genocide'. Bulldozers pushed the bodies into hastily dug mass graves. That too was shown around the world live on television.

Horrified reports by journalists almost immediately prompted an international fundraising campaign. Governments, aid organizations, media concerns, churches of all denominations, foundations, associations, charities and schools, as well as sympathetic individuals in dozens of Western countries, stepped forward to help the 'cholera victims'.

As more money became available, more humanitarian aid organizations came to Goma to help spend it, and with them more journalists to film their rescue efforts.

They held daily press conferences chaired by a representative of the UN High Commission for Refugees. He would introduce each NGO in turn to give an account of what was happening. 'Each one would give a higher death toll, because each one would know that the man with the highest death toll would get on the nine o'clock news that night. And being on the nine o'clock news meant you got money and that is how the NGOs were trying to manipulate the media in Goma,' said Richard Dowden, director of the Royal African Society in London, in a lecture delivered to the London School of Economics on 17 January 2007. He had visited Goma at the time as a journalist working for the *Independent*.

What the aid organizations and journalists failed to mention was that some of the dead in Goma had not succumbed to cholera but had been murdered by Hutu militias, on suspicion of disloyalty. They were accused of planning to return to Rwanda. Any Hutus who wanted to go back to cockroach-land were cockroaches themselves and must be killed, was the reasoning. No autopsies were carried out on the corpses wrapped in rags that vanished into mass graves, but the results of random sampling suggested that in the first month of the crisis alone, 4,000 people were beaten or stabbed to death.

The fact that international extradition warrants were circulating for the *génocidaires* in Goma barely made it into the newspapers either. The Hutus were presented to the public in the West mainly as innocent victims of the cholera bacterium. Perhaps aid organizations and journalists felt a need to make amends. When the genocide broke out, all but a few of the Westerners in Rwanda had packed their bags. In their passionate pleas for help for the cholera victims, who came from the very Rwanda that they had recently left to its fate, aid workers and journalists may have seen a chance to show their more 'humanitarianly correct' side. The presentation of events in press reports and on television took the form of a 'dramatic well-publicized show of human suffering in which the enemy was a virus and the saviour humanitarian aid. An [. . .] emergency in which there was no good or bad side, only victims,' wrote Fiona Terry, project leader of the French arm of Médecins sans Frontières in the region at the time.[1]

The results of the worldwide fundraising campaign broke records: for immediate relief alone a total of $1.5 billion was collected. Donor governments gave the UN refugee organization UNHCR and the humanitarian aid organizations affiliated to it $1 million a day to spend, while another $1 million a day, according to the best estimates, poured in through private channels. The rescue operation mounted for the Hutus became the best-funded humanitarian operation in the world. Even long afterwards, aid organizations would refer to those first few months of the 'cholera crisis' as a period when the 'tap was turned on' and it was possible 'to do anything', which included treating cholera and dysentery with expensive drugs that were unavailable anywhere else in Africa and airlifting clean drinking water all the way from Europe to Goma.[2]

In the blink of an eye aid workers established twenty-five refugee camps large and small around the town of Goma. Pegs for hundreds of thousands of tents were driven into the hard volcanic soil. Thousands of latrines and wells were dug; mountains of corrugated iron were used to build storage depots; clinics and food distribution centres were set up; and kilometres of tarmac were laid in and around the tented camps for intensive use by tankers and trucks.

Before the Goma crisis people were amazed if forty, sometimes as many as eighty, international aid organizations arrived at the scene of a humanitarian disaster, but no fewer than 250 threw themselves into the aid operation in the Great Lakes Region, along with eight UN departments, more than twenty donor governments and institutions, and an untold number of local aid organizations financed by foreign donors. A hundred of the 250 INGOs had chosen Goma as their only field of operations. Never before had so many aid workers been gathered together in a single 'humanitarian territory'.

A year after the start of the 'cholera crisis', a sea of flags bearing the logos of aid organizations was still fluttering over the hundreds of thousands of huts made of blue-and-white UNHCR tarpaulins. The flags had once been intended to make clear to warring factions that humanitarian rather than military organizations were at work. In Goma they were ammunition in a PR war between aid organizations. Then there were the adverts on T-shirts and baseball caps worn by the thousands of aid workers in the camps and on the doors of their fleets of vehicles; water pumps and latrine doors were plastered with company stickers, and in front of office tents and corrugated-iron clinics and orphanages posts were hammered into the ground to hold painted signs bearing the names of the organizations in charge. There were even sticking plasters with the Médecins sans Frontières logo. At such a humanitarian mega-happening, just being there isn't enough. For an aid organization it's at least as important to show that you're there, to avoid being upstaged by the competition.

I saw flags with the logo of the World Health Organization (WHO) and flags bearing the symbols of the UN Children's Fund (UNICEF), the International Organization for Migration (IOM) and the World Food Programme (WFP). I recognized the colours of the International Federation of Red Cross and Red Crescent Societies (IFRC) on signs and banners, but I'd had no idea that organizations called GTZ, THW, AICF, AMD, CAFOD, OFDA, CRS and CEPZa/CELZa existed. Oxfam, Merlin, Equilibre, Trócaire, GOAL and Concern were there, as were CARE Canada and CARE Germany, the Dutch, German and Spanish arms of Caritas, the Swedish Rescue Board, the Order of Malta, Solidarités, Italian Emergency, German Emergency Doctors and the French,

Belgian and Dutch branches of Médecins sans Frontières. Church communities worldwide were represented by the Medical Missionaries of Mary, Samaritan's Purse, the Lutheran World Federation and Christian Aid. I also saw ActionAid, Food for the Poor, Refugee Help, Terre des Hommes, Help the Aged, Feed the Children and Save the Children.

'I tried to imagine an exhausted refugee staggering into Goma, overwhelmed by this astounding display of marketing. I imagined him thinking: "Right, I'll have breakfast with CARE. Then lunch with World Vision, then I'll pop across and collect some medicine from the Red Cross and then collect some plastic sheeting and a blanket and bed down with UNHCR,"' journalist Richard Dowden remarked in the *Independent* on 4 September 1994. In Goma he'd felt as if he were in an 'aid agency supermarket' in which aid groups 'blare[d] out their names and logos like soft drink manufacturers'.

By April 1995 Camp Mugunga had been in existence for a year and it was humming. Bulldozers had turned narrow stony paths into boulevards, which criss-crossed 'residential' and 'business' districts. On either side of the Boulevard de l'Egalité, Rue de la Solidarité and Avenue de la Fraternité were huts that had become more comfortable with every passing month since the arrival of the Hutus and now seemed indestructible. Some *blendés*, as the huts were called, were three storeys high and decoratively overgrown with creepers. They seemed intended for permanent occupation. Goma's volcanic soil was hard but fertile. In fields walled off with blocks of lava, residents were growing potatoes, cabbages, beans and bananas. Other camp-dwellers were tending goats and chickens, and almost everyone had started a tiny ornamental front garden to grow flowers.

By no means all the plastic UNHCR tarpaulins, distributed as standard equipment to every refugee on arrival, were still being used to keep the hundreds of thousands of thatched dwellings dry under the daily downpours of this wettest part of East Africa. Cut into strips they flapped festively from the straw gables of huts with several rooms. Doors were made of flattened cooking-oil tins. The refugee tarpaulins also served as tablecloths in the countless camp restaurants and were hung up as cheerful wallpaper in disco huts. Café Champs-Elysées ran a garden restaurant. When I arrived a goat was marinating on the path outside. Halfway along the Avenue de la Paix et de la Justice patrons were playing noisy games of dominoes at tables in front of the entrances to Bar Patience and Chez Papa Bon. The pungent aroma of marijuana drifted out through the open doors.

Rich and poor Hutus lived separately in different areas, just as they did back home in the villages and towns of Rwanda. On muddy soccer pitches between the various districts they played passionate friendly matches, and there were churches – several hundred of them, since Hutus are devout Catholics. Film enthusiasts could take their seats in one of the many Salles de Spectacle for 1,000 Rwandan francs, roughly 60 euro cents, to enjoy a video show. Golden oldies were playing that week. I saw posters for *Rambo* and *Midnight Express*, no less popular in Goma than they had been at cinemas in Amsterdam and London. The posters were drawn by camp artists. 'Children half price' had been written diagonally across the pictures in marker pen.

The camp economy was flourishing compared to that of Rwanda, where hardly any aid organizations, let alone investors, had shown their faces. Here, in narrow alleyways, the electricians of Mugunga earned a living by repairing radios for their companions in adversity. There were video rental businesses, bakeries, butcher's shops, distilleries and theatres. Barbers advertised their services with paintings of haircuts on cardboard signs and in boutiques women tried on the latest kanga fashions.

I took a tour with a liaison officer from an international team of police who had come to Goma as observers on behalf of the United Nations. Burkina Faso, Benin and Cameroon had each sent a handful of police officers. The man giving me a lift had been loaned to the UN by the Netherlands.

'It's much livelier here than in the villages and towns in Rwanda,' I remarked. We'd stopped in front of a photo-studio hut to admire the family portraits and passport photos on the wall. The studio was directly opposite Hôtel du Monde, where visiting family members, friends and relatives of Hutus could spend the night.

'Everything you see here has been stolen from Rwanda by the Hutus. And you're surprised there's not much going on over there any more?' the policeman muttered.

In fully loaded cars and trucks, on hand-carts, in wheelbarrows, and on the baggage racks of bicycles and mopeds, the Hutus fleeing to Goma had taken with them everything in their home country that wasn't nailed down. Having first killed the owners. Sheets of corrugated iron from Rwandan roofs, furniture, mattresses, toilet bowls, basins – everything was hauled off to the refugee camps. People arrived leading stolen cows and goats behind them on ropes.

'Many Hutus went back to Rwanda several times in those first few weeks to steal yet more property,' the Dutch policeman told me.

It happened to be maths exam day in Mugunga. Rows of students sitting on planks laid across blocks of black lava were solving differential equations with apparent ease. Their teachers, several of whom had worked at the university in Rwanda before fleeing to Goma, peered over their heavy horn-rimmed glasses to make sure nobody was cheating. They were no fools.

The policeman was watching the youngsters too, thoughtfully, as they pencilled in numbers or rubbed them out.

'They've lugged just about the whole university library out of Rwanda with them,' he said after a while. 'That's great for these boys and girls. They can simply go on studying here. But the Tutsi children in Rwanda who survived the massacre have no books any more and no teachers either, because if the teachers were Tutsis they're probably dead and if they were Hutus they're here. Watching these youngsters doing their exams I ask myself yet again what exactly we're up to with our humanitarian aid.'

He was quiet for a moment. Then he heaved a deep sigh. 'Come on, let's get ourselves a beer.'

'Until we go back to Rwanda, the cockroaches can rule over a graveyard!' a Hutu in the crowd shrieked at a Reuters journalist filming the human river flowing towards Goma. He was lugging an old fridge on his head, stolen from the house of a murdered Tutsi family. The exodus from Rwanda had not been a Hutu retreat but a tactical withdrawal. They hadn't moved to Goma because they were beaten but to avoid defeat: in the refugee camps they were safe from the Tutsi army, which wouldn't follow them over the border. The Hutus had decided to leave a systematically looted Rwanda, scattered with rotting corpses, to the 'cockroaches' until the time came to fight their way back. That was the plan.

Along with the Hutu population, the entire extremist Hutu government had relocated to Goma. The prime minister and his cabinet took up residence in the tourist hotels just outside the town, along the banks of Lake Kivu, and carried on governing from beneath Heineken parasols around the edges of swimming pools. There was no need for them to squabble over government expenditure. At the start of the genocide all the assets of Tutsi account holders had been frozen by the Rwandan National Bank. The extremist Hutu leaders had taken the money with them in hard cash, along with all the buses belonging to Rwanda's national public transport company, which were now shuttling back and forth between the camps carrying paying passengers. They'd also packed up and brought along with them the national coffee stocks and the fuel reserves of the state oil company, Petro-Rwanda.

The ministers of Foreign Affairs, Developmental Cooperation and Defence had simply stayed in their jobs. Only the Minister of the Interior had been given a new portfolio. He'd been appointed Minister for Refugee Affairs.

Likewise transferred to Goma, more or less in their entirety, were the government army and their partners in genocide the Interahamwe citizens' militia, 20,000 –100,000 men in total; estimates varied rather widely. They brought with them the Kalashnikovs, mortars, anti-aircraft missiles, anti-tank grenades, machetes and axes they'd used to murder their Tutsi compatriots. There were even six helicopters and a couple of tanks, parked in between the aid supply warehouses and health clinics run by humanitarian aid agencies. The Hutu-copters were out of commission, incidentally, for lack of spare parts.

Mindful of the Red Cross principles of neutrality and impartiality, the aid organizations in Goma were committed to helping anybody they could. Only four weeks after the cholera crisis began, in August 1994, Oxfam UK made it known that the minimum requirement of five litres of clean drinking water per camp-dweller per day, as laid down in international refugee law, was already available. There were 'no more than 10 faecal coliforms per 100ml at the point of delivery for undisinfected supplies', the organization proudly announced in a press release. Other INGOs declared that the 'nutritional status' of the refugees could be described as 'excellent'.

While aid organizations went on filling a growing number of clinics and food distribution centres with logistics experts, nutritionists, construction engineers, managers, administrators and doctors, the old, extremist Rwanda that had settled undisturbed in Goma was being reborn as a state within a state. The Hutu leaders created *préfectures* in the camps, which they subdivided into *communes* and *secteurs*, which in turn were divided into *quartiers* and *sous-quartiers*, each composed of *cellules* of roughly ten huts. Every *cellule* had an appointed leader, and from among them emerged a *sous-quartier* boss. This meant the Hutus in the camps were kept under extremely tight control by the regime. On all food rations distributed by aid organizations, the Hutu government, from its tourist hotels, levied a 'war tax' to pay its army, which enabled it to continue its campaign of extermination against the Tutsi enemy back in Rwanda. The inhabitants of the camp, now rested, well nourished and inoculated, were a source of new recruits. Inflammatory radio stations based in the camps, staffed by the extremist *Journalistes*

Rwandais en Exil, ensured they were properly motivated.

'Crushing a cockroach isn't murder. It's a hygiene measure!' I heard a voice crackle from transistor radios. Between the *blendés*, vendors hawked the camp newspaper, a rag produced on stolen stencil machines. 'One Cockroach is Sufficient to Cause a Plague' was that day's main front-page headline.

Almost every night, militias crept back over the border into Rwanda to go 'hunting Tutsi'. They struck mercilessly at Zairean Tutsis born in Goma as well. Hundreds of local Tutsis went missing or were found dead with bullets through their hearts or with their throats slit.

The violence perpetrated by the Hutus went unpunished. 'Everyone knows what has to be done, but who will bell the cat?' asked Shahryar Khan, Special Representative of the UN Secretary-General in the Great Lakes Region in November 1994. The Zairean authorities refused to accept any responsibility for security in the camps. The militias needed to be kept away from 'ordinary' camp-dwellers, by force if necessary. UN Secretary-General Boutros Boutros-Ghali suggested sending blue helmets with a robust mandate, but of the sixty UN member states he asked to provide troops, fifty-nine said no. None of them felt like sending their soldiers into the war between Hutus and Tutsis. Nine international military contingents were moving about in the Great Lakes Region, but they were there purely to assist in the battle against cholera. The UN peacekeeping force UNAMIR, units of the French and British armies, the US army with 3,000 GIs operating from bases in Entebbe in Uganda, units large and small from Canada, Australia and the Netherlands, the Japanese Defence Force with around 400 troops and a team from the Israeli army had field hospitals, transport planes and trucks, but no orders to take out a single Hutu extremist. The maxim of their 'humanitarian intervention' in this crisis was neutrality – just like that of the aid organizations. They had no orders to arrest *génocidaires*. As a last resort, the UN eventually took up President Mobutu of Zaire's offer to send his presidential guard to the camps, at the UN's expense. What the

UN feared would happen happened: Mobutu's guards arrived in Goma with *carte blanche* to supplement their UN salaries by means of theft and extortion.

I hadn't been walking around Camp Mugunga for more than half an hour before I was stopped. There were five of them and they held me at gunpoint. They snatched my bag off my shoulder, rummaged around in it and found a pen and a notebook.

'Journalist,' I explained.

'We want presents!' the commander of the group snapped at me. He pointed to the CNN pin on the lapel of his uniform. 'Give us something like this!' My pen disappeared into his pocket. With a 'Watch out for the refugees! They're criminals!' they disappeared into a busy camp alleyway.

I was driven to the exit of Camp Mugunga by the Dutch policeman in his white Land Cruiser. He too regarded a walk among the Hutus as unacceptably dangerous.

'You need a bright light to find any sense of shame or conscience here,' he said. 'Shall I demonstrate?' He wound down the window of his vehicle a cautious seven centimetres and called out through the slit to an approaching Hutu: '*Excusez! Monsieur!* Are you a *génocidaire?*'

The man, in a tattered raincoat that was far too big for him, a small plough over his left shoulder, stopped and stuck his nose through the window opening. He sniffed deeply.

'*Oui,*' he said.

'Why did you murder your fellow countrymen?' asked the policeman. The Hutu sniffed again.

'Just because . . .'

'*Merci et bonjour,*' the policeman said hurriedly and he nudged the accelerator. Then to me: 'See what I mean? And all that lot are walking about freely here. Someone ought to do something.'

A year after the arrival of the Hutus, 'traitors' to the Hutu cause were still being carried into camp clinics with arms or legs hacked off by militias and dead babies were still being pulled out of camp latrines.

'Rape babies,' a member of the IOM told me. He'd fished several out of the cesspits himself.

One year on from the initial influx of refugees, the violence and aggression were still so terrifying that aid workers didn't dare stay in the camps after sunset. They withdrew to the town of Goma until daylight returned.

'It just didn't make sense any more,' wrote Fiona Terry of MSF France. 'All the organizations [. . .] did fantastic work on a technical level but they were unable to protect the refugees from violence. Once we feel that a population risks dying from violence, what are we doing being in a health clinic giving out Panadol?'[3] But every morning the aid workers devoted themselves to their daily humanitarian duties once more.

The Hutus' energy intake demanded urgent attention, for example. Spot checks had indicated that on average it was now too low. It varied from camp to camp, but the number of calories consumed per person per day was between 900 and 1,700, whereas a minimum of 2,045 calories is needed to keep the average person at a healthy weight. The lack of nutrition was in part the result of attacks on food convoys on their way to the camps and the terrorizing of the inhabitants by the militias, who robbed them of their aid rations on distribution days. In their evaluations some INGOs estimated that on average militias stole 60 per cent of all aid supplies being distributed, partly for their own use, partly to sell back to civilians in the camps. At camp markets tins of sardines were on display with 'gift from Japan' on the label, along with piles of stolen jerrycans, sleeping mats, blankets, soap and medicines. The World Food Programme once found a boat on the lake at the entrance to its food warehouse. The crew was calmly loading it with sacks of rice to take to the hotels where members of the government were staying. Fearful of bad publicity and a consequent decline in financial support, the INGOs kept quiet about the thefts. Instead they inflated the number of people living in the camps in reports to their donors, so that the losses would be made up. By contrast, press releases were issued every time the package of humanitarian provision was expanded, by introducing homoeopathic therapies, for example, or psychological support.

A handful of INGOs made half-hearted attempts to prevent the theft of aid goods by hiring security staff. The result was yet more violence. In one attack twenty-five private security guards at an aid supplies warehouse belonging to CARE Canada were shot dead by robbers. Their places at the gate were coolly taken by Hutu extremists, who then demanded – and apparently got – regular salaries from CARE.

Several thousand extremists insisted they be given jobs as drivers, maintenance technicians, administrative staff, cooks, cleaners and managers in the many food and non-food distribution centres run by INGOs, and in their water-supply and building projects, social programmes for orphans and disabled people, and family-reunion and educational services. Hutu leaders in the camps creamed off a percentage of every salary. At one point MSF Belgium was employing 550 Hutu personnel in one of the camps, at an average monthly salary of $100. According to some estimates the Hutu leaders were collecting 'taxes' of $11,000 a month from the staff of that one organization alone.

Charities providing medical treatment hired Hutu nurses for night duty, since it was too dangerous after dark for Western staff. There was no shortage: a substantial proportion of the Rwandan public health system had settled in the camps, including more than a hundred nurses as well as the Minister of Health himself. Fiona Terry later admitted that doctors suspected the night shift of murdering patients who were insufficiently loyal to the Hutu cause. In the morning, when the international staff returned to work, they would find family members or more distant relatives of Hutu leaders in the beds that had become free. When asked where the original patients had gone, the night nurses couldn't say. 'We wondered how many of our Rwandan staff – working in the feeding centre, the hospital, even in our house – had blood on their hands,' she wrote.

'But these thoughts were pushed aside in the daily battles to combat a shigellosis epidemic and rising malnutrition and to minimize the diversion of supplies. They would reappear around the table at night, after a couple of beers.' Terry described Goma as a 'total ethical disaster'. 'Should we respect conventional medical ethics, treating anyone who needed it regardless of their history, or should we recognize our wider responsibility?'[4]

The sun set blood red. Outside Bar Palma Village in the town of Goma I could see the logos of WFP, MSF Belgium, IOM, UNHCR, ICRC and Action contre la Faim on white Land Cruisers. Inside the bar sat the Western staffs of those organizations, letting their hair down after yet another day in the camps. Traditional Belgian beer was poured 'stiff and wet'. Bougainvillaea grew in thick clusters right through the walls.

The local Zairean authorities had recently introduced a curfew. Opinions differed as to the reason. Was the ban on going out at night intended to make laying mines more difficult or easier? Either way, those gathered here would need to make sure they were drunk by seven in the evening. Anyone found outdoors after that time risked losing his work permit and being expelled from the country.

'What exactly was the problem between Tutsis and Hutus about? And what's the problem now?' I asked no one in particular.

My table companions shrugged. 'You'll have to ask the politicians. It's not our concern,' one of them said.

A member of the WFP staff changed the subject: 'I had yet another of those meetings with the camp mayors today.' He stared into his glass dejectedly. 'Nothing but complaints. No more white beans in the rations, they had to be brown beans, and the maize meal was too thick. "What time would you like to eat from now on and would you perhaps like a Waldorf salad with your dinner?" I asked at one point, but my sarcasm escaped them. They'd discuss the salad with their bosses, they said.'

And did I imagine anyone ever said thank you? 'Ha!' sneered the WFP guy. 'On the contrary! We're given orders to deliver firewood in lengths of exactly sixty centimetres in future.'

'Let AIDS take care of them!' said someone who was listening from the table behind us, raising his glass.

'And Ebola!' roared another aid worker.

'May the Nyarangongo erupt!'

'Hear, hear,' came the cry.

'Look, for you, a nice T-shirt with our logo on it,' said a member of the IOM as we parted at five to seven.

I spent the remainder of my time in Goma, before walking back to the border the following morning, being entertained in my room by the French television station TV5, which was broadcasting a figure-skating championship. All night I watched finalists performing triple jumps in glittering costumes.

Epilogue

An inventory of the four main camps in Goma at the end of 1995 rendered up: 2,324 bars, 450 restaurants, 590 shops, over 60 hair salons, 50 pharmacies, 30 tailors, 25 butcher's shops, 5 blacksmiths, 4 photo studios, 3 cinemas, 2 hotels and an abattoir.

A week or so after I left, a Hercules flew in from Germany to Goma with its hold full of cuddly toys spontaneously collected by German schoolchildren. The same day a planeload of munitions landed. It wasn't the first weapons delivery the Hutus had received, UN inspectors said. Arms dealers were routinely paid in cash by Hutu leaders, although sometimes weapons were bartered for stolen aid supplies.

To the great discomfort of the international humanitarian community, aid to Goma was terminated after two years, in November 1996. The Rwandan Tutsi army invaded Goma, drove out all the

INGOs, fired on the camps until they were empty and burned the tents and clinics to the ground. Anyone who was paying attention would have known it was going to happen. Rwanda had warned the international aid community from the start that if no one did anything to end the dangerous regrouping in Goma of the perpetrators of genocide, close to the border with Rwanda, then they would. But even two years after the crisis began, new aid organizations were still arriving to fill the last little gaps in the humanitarian safety net. With the help of Artistes sans Frontières, for example, camp residents who wished to do so could learn to become creditable weavers of baskets and mats.

Several thousand inhabitants of the camps were killed during the eviction campaigns by the Rwandan Tutsi army. That was the fault of the aid organizations, the Rwandan president, Paul Kagame, told a journalist from the *New Yorker* with a shrug. 'I think we should start blaming these people,' he said, referring to the aid agencies, 'who actually supported these camps – spent one million dollars per day in these camps, gave support to these groups to rebuild themselves into a force. [. . .] Why shouldn't we accuse them?'[5]

Around 600,000 Hutus made the trek on foot back to Rwanda, but 200,000 militants and their families fled deeper into the bush. There, in what is now the Democratic Republic of Congo, they still remain.

In 1998 Rwanda invaded Congo again. This time it touched off a war that lasted five years and drew the armies of four other nations into Congo. In what became known as Africa's First World War, an alliance of Ugandan and Rwandan military forces along with Congolese rebel groups took control of much of Congo's north and east, while the armies of Zimbabwe, Angola and Namibia intervened to defend Congo's capital, Kinshasa, from the invaders.

In 2002, at the urging of the UN, a peace accord was signed. It is still violated almost daily by all parties. Rwandan Hutu militias are a core factor in the bloodletting in central Africa. So far, up to the year 2010, an estimated 5 million lives were lost.

Most television viewers in the West failed to notice exactly how, if at all, the 'cholera crisis' in Goma ended, and the procession of humanitarian aid organizations largely moved on. Victims of wars in Liberia, Sudan, Iraqi Kurdistan and Afghanistan urgently needed their help.

2. Contract fever

*For the aid organizations in Goma it was a matter of feed
the killers or go under as an organization.*

An aid worker in Goma

Abundant humanitarian aid was all that enabled the Hutu extremists
to carry on their extermination campaign against the Tutsis in
Rwanda from UNHCR camps in Goma. The Hutu government
in exile had few if any other sources of income, apart from the
capital it had stolen. Without humanitarian aid, the Hutus' war
would almost certainly have ground to a halt fairly quickly. No
one has ever called the aid industry to account for its role in the
conflict, least of all the aid organizations themselves; the international humanitarian community is convinced that the causes and
effects of both war and aid are the responsibility of politicians. Aid
organizations in Goma claimed neutrality in the conflict between
Hutus and Tutsis, insisting they were in Goma to relieve human
suffering and nothing else.

'Most of us gave no thought at all to the ethics of our aid
provision,' a member of staff at an American organization called
Refugee Help confessed later. The aid agencies in Goma were in
the grip of 'contract fever'. 'It's perhaps embarrassing to admit,
but much of the discussion between headquarters and the field
focused on contracts [to implement donor projects]: securing them,
maintaining them, and increasing them. The pressure was on: Get
more contracts! How many contracts did we have? When were they
up? What were the chances that they would be renewed? Were there
any competitors?'[1]

The battle for contracts that went on between organizations was
paramount, and among other things it prevented them from joining
forces to combat Hutu violence and the theft of aid supplies.

Attempts by a few INGOs to get back on track ethically were promptly exploited by rival organizations. An Irish aid agency, for example, tried to cut down on luxuries at a camp where many Hutu leaders had settled by refusing to hand out any more soap or mattresses. Competing organizations immediately rushed to fill the gap in the market by pouring their own mattresses and soap into it.

Another example: aid organizations were not prepared to supply food to Camp Panzi and Camp Bulonge, since they were inhabited almost exclusively by Hutu soldiers. The Catholic organization Caritas decided to take these particular projects upon itself. 'They need to eat; they're not all murderers,' it said. Later Caritas would claim that the supplying of food to Panzi and Bulonge had been a preventive measure. By filling soldiers' stomachs, Caritas had been trying to put a stop to the theft of food from other, 'innocent' refugees.[2]

The Hutu extremists were able to pursue a strategy of divide and rule. The INGOs were their willing captives. While some INGOs in Goma cut back on their Hutu staffs to reduce the opportunities for the militias to cream off salaries, rival organizations took on more Hutus to ease relations with Hutu leaders. And the moment one aid organization decided to start paying salaries to its Hutu employees in local currency rather than dollars, sabotaging the currency exchange businesses run by camp leaders, another would do exactly the opposite, switching from local currency to payment in dollars.

In a Hutu camp on the far side of the lake, on Tanzanian soil, the UNHCR decided to finance projects by no more than twelve different INGOs in an effort to reduce the opportunities for Hutu leaders to play one organization off against another. Aid agencies not selected by the UNHCR promptly pitched their tents outside the camp and did all they could to entice Hutus there with larger food parcels, warmer blankets and a broader selection of free pharmaceuticals. There weren't quite enough of them to cause utter chaos.

As one of a hundred aid organizations in Goma, it would be pointless to close down your aid project and leave in protest at the violence and the abuse of aid supplies, said an aid worker. 'No one would have paid any attention if we left. They would have just carried on without us.'[3]

In December 1994 MSF France nevertheless did decide to leave Goma. In a newsletter sent out to its individual donors the organization wrote: 'Far from contributing to a solution, aid only perpetuates the situation in Goma.'[4]

Their fellow aid workers were far from appreciative of MSF France's public criticism of the aid operation. The Dutch, Swiss and Spanish branches of MSF coolly invalidated the claim of their French colleagues that the situation in Goma had become 'untenable' by taking over the work of MSF France. MSF Belgium added insult to injury by saying that the 'political signal' the French said they wanted to send by leaving was inspired in part by the assessment that their project in Goma was finished in any case. In presenting its motives for leaving Goma as an ethical *tour de force*, the Belgians sneered, MSF France was simply trying to generate publicity for what it would have done anyway.

Nor was the relationship between MSF France and the UNHCR, an important source of contracts for all branches of MSF, exactly improved by the departure of the French. MSF France had jeopardized the favourable fundraising climate in Europe and the US by offering a glimpse behind the scenes of the 'refugee crisis'. Like any ordinary humanitarian aid organization, the UNHCR has no money of its own but is entirely dependent for its continued existence on what donors wish to contribute when a humanitarian drama develops. 'We can shout and scream, and they may listen . . . or they may not,' was how former UN Secretary-General Boutros-Ghali described the financial reality for all UN organizations. A UNHCR spokesman in Geneva repeated to journalists the malicious suggestion that the departure of MSF France had little to do with principled objections. It was late December. 'Our own people would have preferred to be home for Christmas too.'

The UNHCR asked MSF France how they could rely on MSF in future.[5] They needn't have worried. In the new millennium too, the various branches of MSF are important implementing partners for the UNHCR.

'There's a market for good works, and it's big business. Call it the "moral economy" if you like,' Nicholas Stockton, a former executive director of Oxfam, told *Newsweek*.[6] We see what looks like one big happy family moving in concert into crisis zones to ease human suffering, but the most powerful link between humanitarian aid agencies is that of commercial competition. Wars and disasters generally attract a garish array of individual organizations, each with its own agenda, its own business imperatives and institutional survival tactics. It's a long time now since the relief of suffering was something the humanitarian world engaged in wearing exercise sandals. Nowadays, as the aid workers themselves point out, they dress in sharp business suits. Organizations that want to remain competitive need to know all about integrated marketing strategies, cost-benefit analyses and competitive incentives. Ideally their top management will be made up of graduates trained in non-profit management or business economics, with an understanding of product positioning, proposal development and client relations. There is no sign of donor fatigue; the budgets of donor governments and contributions from private donors grow every year, as does the number of aid agencies wanting to help spend the billions donated, and the competition between them.[7]

Aid organizations that fail to put in an appearance at each new humanitarian disaster miss out on contracts for the implementation of aid projects financed by donor governments and institutions, and are bypassed left, right and centre by competing organizations that do show up. Whether it's a matter of the construction and supplying of refugee camps and orphanages, the repair of bombed roads and buildings, the disarming and re-education of child soldiers, or the inoculation of entire populations against polio, the INGOs that send official donors the most competitive bids for

the huge amount of work involved will come out on top in the
tendering process.

Start-up costs in distant crisis-hit countries are sky high. Aid
organizations have to recruit and hire staff, rent and furnish
housing and office space, and bring in materials and equipment,
such as Land Cruisers, aid supplies, satellite dishes, computers,
air-conditioners, office equipment and generators. Once at work
in a 'humanitarian territory', INGOs have to ensure they can
remain active there for as long as it takes to earn back their investments at the very least. Generally speaking this is possible only
if they can win further contracts *in situ* and extend their existing
agreements. Contracts with donors are always short term: three
to six months is common. When called upon to pay for emergency
aid in conflict zones, where no one on the ground knows for
certain what the situation will look like tomorrow, if they are still
there at all, donors have a preference for projects that can be
carried out quickly and, if their luck holds, without encountering
any problems or criticism.

The more income they receive in a crisis zone, the better able
INGOs are to prepare themselves for newly emerging disasters.
With more staff and more gear they can respond more rapidly.
This is crucial. INGOs that are already successfully carrying out
projects in crisis zones have the best chance of securing future
assignments.

If more donor contracts are available for a crisis elsewhere, then
the procession of humanitarian aid organizations has to move on
there as quickly as possible. When donors redirected the flow of
money, aid organizations exchanged the sufferings of the people
of Sierra Leone in 2001–2 for those of the Afghans, and the refugee
camps in Darfur in 2004–5 for the reception camps in tsunami
regions. Far from worrying mainly about how the local population
will survive when a contract runs out, the contract system means
aid organizations are forced to worry instead about how they'll
survive themselves.

★

The best way for INGOs to attract attention is through the media. Coverage of disasters on television and in the newspapers is crucial to humanitarian operational management.

Former UN Secretary-General Boutros-Ghali more than once referred to the television station CNN as 'the sixteenth member of the Security Council'. Without its broadcast images, donor governments would take no action at all. Media attention is no guarantee; plenty of harrowing stories have appeared in the newspapers and on television without leading to significant support from donors, while other humanitarian operations were well underway before any media attention was paid to them. But no one denies there is a link between publicity and interest among donors, and it has existed for a long time. Remember 1968. Hunger in Biafra. 'I don't care what you do. Just get those goddamn nigger babies off my TV screen!' President Lyndon Johnson thundered at his spin doctors. He wanted to prevent publicity about Biafra leading to pressure on politicians to act.

Significant proportions of aid organizations' budgets are devoted to 'press and publicity'. 'At one time,' journalist Richard Dowden wrote in the *Economist* of 2 July 2001, 'organizations like the Red Cross were too exalted to talk to journalists. In the early 1980s in Beirut I was told by the Red Cross chief to telephone their headquarters in Geneva if I wanted to know what they were doing in Lebanon. All that changed in the late 1980s when the aid business took off. [. . .] Several NGOs employed attractive young women as press officers.'

This early period also gave rise to the following explanation by George Alagiah on BBC television in 1992 about the famine in Somalia: 'Relief agencies depend upon us for publicity and we need them to tell us where the stories are. There's an unspoken understanding between us, a sort of code. We try not to ask the question too bluntly: "Where will we find the starving babies?" And they never answer explicitly. We get the pictures just the same.'

Aid organizations clamber aboard when the media set out to capture audiences. The size of their readership increasingly preoccupies journalists. Pieter Broertjes, editor-in-chief of Dutch newspaper *Volkskrant*, finds this only natural. 'Every hour we lose four subscribers,' he said.[8]

Four years after the Goma crisis the British Secretary of State for International Development, Clare Short, described the journalists she had seen at work in Goma at the time as 'chasing each other's tails for the next story'. 'How could people living in the refugee camps have understood the mutual parasitism of the media and the fundraiser? They asked for bread, and we gave them a circus.'[9] More media attention to disasters and crises means more income for aid agencies. Being the only one to decline to take part in humanitarian hype would be pointless; the circus would simply go on without your organization.

Ten years after Goma, Lei Brouns, a Dutch member of staff at the NGO Terre des Hommes, was in the tsunami-affected region of Sri Lanka. He watched the media circus with a sinking feeling. 'The past few months I've seen aid organizations from the United States, Taiwan and South Korea lay their banners and logos over Terre des Hommes projects and then film and photograph them. At moments like that I sometimes ask myself where on earth we've ended up with this job and this line of work.'[10]

The old-established aid organizations often lose out to the new boys in the race for publicity. The venerable International Red Cross sometimes finds this extremely galling, since it's always been obliged to go wherever help is needed, often in the face of considerable hazard, whereas an organization like Médecins sans Frontières may decide to go or may not. The ICRC can't match the publicity that results from the 'cool MTV atmosphere' surrounding MSF, a spokesperson complained. 'We don't make a spectacle of our departure for a disaster zone, the way the media like. Everyone takes it for granted we'll go. Unfortunately we've learned from MSF that you have to sell yourself as well.'[11]

Savvy aid organizations have journalists embedded with them to witness humanitarian dramas. They offer the press free flights.

On the ground they're ready to provide chauffeur-driven cars and interpreters. Bed and board for journalists may be on offer as well. Reporter W. F. Deedes of the *Daily Telegraph* wrote: 'I have struck a number of such bargains in recent years. In return for the lift, I make mention in this newspaper of the work being done by the organization working to relieve the human condition. It becomes part of the story.'[12]

Increasingly, reporters wanting to go to a crisis zone are given the go-ahead by their bosses as long as an aid organization pays for the trip. Dutch photographer Ad van Denderen complained on Dutch Radio 1 about the declining willingness of editorial boards to invest in reporting from 'far-off countries'. 'Dutch photographers' biggest clients nowadays are aid organizations,' he claimed.[13] The presenter of the radio programme didn't respond to what Van Denderen had said. A cosy relationship between NGOs and journalists, whether they work for radio, television or the newspapers, has become the norm, and that relationship undoubtedly has a financial side.

Whether you're with *NOS Journaal*, the main Dutch evening news programme, the regular documentary *Eén Vandaag*, whose journalists were led around Liberia by Dutch MSF, *Netwerk*, which made the same trip but with the Dutch refugee charity Stichting Vluchteling, or the BBC that travelled through Sierra Leone with Oxfam, having an aid organization guide you through a crisis zone is like looking at Europe through the eyes of the Salvation Army. With a saucepan of soup and a Salvationist, the camera crew treks past half-frozen people sleeping in doorways and crack-addicted teenage mothers.

The journalists' trips take them to crushingly hopeless *post-bellum* territory. The chosen backdrops more or less speak for themselves: homes for war orphans, aid projects for amputees and feeding stations for the starving. Not a single healthy person features in their reports, aside from white aid workers. Africans are guaranteed to be shown tottering half naked through crammed refugee camps. They have nothing to do but wait for Western aid. Children have flies in their eyes and swollen bellies and mothers have breasts like used tea bags. Victims are universal and stripped of anything that might frighten off donors, such as political convictions or tainted pasts. They're the obvious good guys: 'women and children', 'the elderly and babies', 'defenceless civilians'. In these stories they do what you'd expect victims to do. They suffer, full stop.

To prevent donors from falling prey to an I've-seen-it-before syndrome, aid workers and journalists often reach for superlatives. Readers repeatedly find themselves looking at a new 'greatest humanitarian crisis in recent history'. Meanwhile, human misery is subject to devaluation as the drama of its presentation increases. To hold the attention of its zapping viewers, CNN managed to trump genocide. The reporter spoke of the 'deadly genocide of 1994'.[14]

'The international development establishment is rigging the game to make Africa – which is, of course, still very poor – look even worse than it really is,' writes developmental economist William Easterly. 'What percentage of the African population would you say dies in war every year? What share of male children, age 10 to 17, are child soldiers? How many Africans are afflicted by famine or died of AIDS last year or are living as refugees? In each case, the answer is one-half of 1% of the population or less. In some cases it's much less.'[15]

Exaggeration has become the norm, said Marcel Vos, head of marketing and communications for Dutch MSF, as long ago as 1997:

> Dutch MSF unnecessarily exaggerated the misery in its reports about the eviction of refugees from the camps in Goma in November 1996. 'We are guilty of carelessly bandying figures about,' Vos says. In the magazine *Sponsorship and Fundraising* he points to a figure of more than a million victims. 'That arose from the feeling: here's a disaster so great that you can't tackle it on your own as an aid organization. You need large-scale military logistics. International intervention. And then a figure of ten thousand victims comes over as less convincing than a million or even more.' Fundraisers use figures the way they are used in

the world of advertising, where hyperbole is a way of selling products, Vos claims. 'I wonder whether this is a matter of an ethical dilemma or shrewdness.' [16]

After all the publicity surrounding the crisis, Dutch MSF received the equivalent of €400,000 in private donations.

In the stories they sponsor, aid organizations are shown doing what they can, but the threat of mass fatalities remains, since resources are limited and supply routes pot-holed. There must be no glimmer of hope for the victims' future, otherwise people will put their coins in someone else's collecting tin. If aid has arrived it's dismissed in the same paragraph as 'too little too late'.

Do aid workers use journalists? Of course they do, said Jacques de Milliano, former director of Dutch MSF. 'To raise funds. It's the job of journalists to provide balanced reporting, to refuse to prostitute themselves to aid organizations. There ought to be an element of journalistic pride.'[17]

Journalism seems to be moving in precisely the opposite direction. Costs are cut and standards eroded by media proprietors, resulting in what the British journalist Nick Davies in his book *Flat Earth News* calls 'churnalism', in other words 'journalists failing to perform the simple basic functions of their profession; quite unable to tell their readers the truth about what is happening on their patch. This is journalists who are no longer out gathering news but who are reduced instead to passive processors of whatever material comes their way, churning out stories, whether real event or PR artifice, important or trivial, true or false.'[18]

It's apparently so easy for the PR departments of aid organizations to get their own agendas on to the television and into the newspapers as 'news' that some have found it necessary to impose some self-restraint. As early as 1994, at the start of the genocide in Rwanda, several of the world's largest aid organizations signed up to a code of conduct intended to govern communication with the press and the public. It was compiled by the International Federation of Red Cross and Red Crescent Societies. Signatories to the code agreed that in their briefings, publicity and advertising they would acknowledge victims of disasters to be 'dignified human beings, not hopeless objects'.

But if your competitors act otherwise and raise money as a result, you have no choice but to join them.

Confronted with humanitarian disasters, journalists who usually like to present themselves as objective outsiders suddenly become the disciples of aid workers. They accept uncritically the humanitarian aid agencies' claims to neutrality, elevating the trustworthiness and expertise of aid workers above journalistic scepticism.

But the most important factor perpetuating this intimacy between aid workers and journalists is that most journalists see nothing wrong in it. Quite the opposite. It's all in a good cause, right? What could possibly be wrong with drawing attention to a good cause?

3. MONGOs

You aren't allowed to be amateurish if you are in the game of saving lives. The one human right that the poor and the vulnerable should have at the very least is to be protected from incompetence.

Jan Egeland, United Nations Undersecretary-General for Humanitarian Affairs and Emergency Relief Coordinator (2003–7)[1]

In the swimming pool beside the neatly laid tables at the Mamba Point restaurant in Freetown that evening, white women were being taught water aerobics and the conference hall near the entrance was hosting the seminar 'The Traumatized Child'. Mantovani's strings played around us, ice-cubes tinkled in our glasses of white wine, and waiters slunk about with bowls of sauce and steaming platters.

· The salaries, per diems and danger-and-discomfort bonuses on offer make working in the established aid sector highly attractive. In 'humanitarian territories', the restaurants, squash courts and golf and tennis facilities are often back up and running before bombed-out schools and clinics. With three-quarters of Sierra Leone still in the hands of murderous rebels and the majority of the population wandering the region crazed with fear, humanitarians were able to wield their clubs and racquets once more on the raked greens and gravel of the capital, Freetown.

It was summer 2002, a year after the signing of the peace accord. We had steak, on the menu at 47,000 leones, the equivalent of €15. That was over half a month's salary for the waiters serving us, the UNICEF representative to my left at the table told me.

'If this meal were to cost half the amount *we* earn per month, we'd be in for a bill of at least five thousand euro a head, not including the wine,' calculated the representative of WHO.

Apart from the waiters, the only Africans inside the restaurant compound or indeed anywhere near it, were chauffeurs for the humanitarians dining there. They waited patiently outside the restaurant. Now and then one of their bosses would send a doggy bag their way. Only a minority of those involved in aid programmes are local people, and they're mostly interpreters, nannies or drivers. At an analytical and policymaking level at least, the overwhelming majority of the staff of international aid organizations are white Westerners. As a rule, Sierra Leoneans in Freetown can barely even get close to the white humanitarians. At the gates to the white community's homes, offices, hotels, clubs and restaurants the security guards are armed with batons, sometimes guns, for chasing away uninvited locals.

For three full years Sierra Leone was in favour with international donors, and humanitarian organizations there received the largest number of donated dollars per head of population. Where all that money was going puzzled me, since the United Nations Development Programme had recently declared Sierra Leone, yet again, to be the world's poorest country.

'How do people actually survive here?' I asked my dining companions. I was eager to hear their response. After all, I was sitting with the captains of the aid industry: donors, consultants to donors, and INGO top managers.

They exchanged glances that said, 'Any ideas?'

Then they all burst into ebullient laughter. 'Juju!' they cried in unison – sorcery.

'Come on, let's pop another bottle of wine, guys,' the European Commission representative shouted above the jovial hubbub.

The humanitarian aid community that travels to war-torn, crisis-ridden countries feels no embarrassment about looking like an international jet set on holiday. Its Land Cruisers can be found triple-parked outside the restaurants, bars and discos of war-ravaged towns and cities every evening. Wherever aid workers go, prostitution instantly soars. I've often seen bar stools occupied by white agronomists, millennium-objective experts or gender-studies consultants with local teenage girls in their laps. I've known aid workers who cared for child soldiers and war orphans by day and relaxed by night in the arms of child prostitutes.

These bad impressions are further reinforced by the endless conferences, by top managers who use business-class flights to get around the globe, by humanitarian territories where you can't move for aid workers because they've all headed for the same disaster, and by the lack of results. Which all helps to explain why a growing number of concerned Western citizens think they can do better and decide to set up their own aid organizations. MONGOs, they're called: 'My Own NGO'. MONGOs make up what has become a vast counter-movement, run by people who are convinced they can get things sorted out in a crisis zone more effectively, quickly and cheaply than the 'real' aid workers with – to MONGO eyes at least – self-serving motives and cumbrous bureaucracy.

When MONGOs head for the humanitarian dramas that are making the TV headlines at home, they do so fired by the passionate conviction that the established aid organizations have yet again reacted too late, that 'as always' they've delivered too few aid supplies and on arrival have 'done nothing, except drive their Land Cruisers at speed past their aid projects, or to the local bars'. Each Land Cruiser costs roughly what it would take to build an orphanage somewhere, MONGOs calculate, and for the price of a full tank of petrol you could probably run the place for a year.

The 'ladies' auxiliary committees' and 'isolated enthusiasts' that Henri Dunant watched dabbling on the battlefield at Solferino in 1859 are experiencing a renaissance in the form of MONGOs. As a direct result of their lack of knowledge and experience, Dunant lobbied for the establishment of a professional aid organization. His International Red Cross became a reality but the MONGOs remained. And multiplied. As Dunant knew, every human being possesses 'the humane desire to lighten a little the torments of all these poor wretches'.

The animosity is mutual. 'Cowboys', the traditional aid organizations sneer; 'little amateur Red Crosses', 'disaster groupies', 'airy-fairy organizations'. The threshold outsiders have to cross to gain access to humanitarian territories is too low, they complain. But the fact is, humanitarian aid exists in a free market, where anyone who chooses to can set up a stall.

Whoever feels like it can establish an organization and start collecting money. In many businesses the staff donate a few per cent of their monthly salaries to charity and local councils will 'adopt' a village in a disaster zone. Housewives are requested to hand over their empty deposit bottles at supermarket entrances, and bridge clubs and choirs organize raffles, jumble sales and goods donations.

According to the ICRC, 'well-intended but unwanted gifts that clog up airfields and logistical hubs' are among the most significant problems faced by anyone providing emergency relief in a crisis. Standard deliveries from MONGO collectors that arrive at pretty much every disaster area and crisis zone include shipping containers full of cast-off equipment from Western hospitals, often broken or set to the wrong voltage, and drugs made available free of charge by pharmaceutical companies after passing their sell-by dates.

At least as inevitable are shipments of second-hand toys and used clothing. Great heaps of clothes were dumped at the roadsides on the way to tsunami territory, unwanted by survivors who'd already been given enough to wear for the rest of their lives or had rejected garments that didn't comply with their cultural rules. Tsunami victims were further bemused by the arrival of crates of winter coats, polar tents, stiletto-heeled court shoes, G-strings for women and packets of Viagra. Bosnians received consignments of Prozac – a little past their sell-by date but some say quite welcome all the same. 'The Greek Orthodox Church organisation Solidarity admitted it might have sent unsuitable relief clothing to tsunami victims, responding to accusations that Father Christmas costumes, fur coats and skimpy women's underwear were among donations to Sri Lanka. "It cannot be ruled out that, through negligence, volunteers sent a few bundles containing totally useless items," Solidarity said to AFP.'[2]

Overzealous MONGOs have been known to ship frostbite medication to victims of tropical disasters, and starving Somalis received laxatives, slimming cures and electric blankets. Above the camps near Goma one day, an enthusiastic individual pushed crates out of an aircraft. Eye-witnesses claim the Hutus found inside them, among other things, ski gloves and rotten cheese.

In Kosovo in 1999, dozens of foreign aid organizations handed out food, clothing and pharmaceuticals to every Kosovar they came upon in the street, without waiting to be asked. Cambodian refugees were sent a shipment of food so old that the director of a zoo in San Francisco had declared it unfit for the animals, and a New Zealand manufacturer offered Kenyan children a shipment of canned dog food. 'The children are hungry, but not *that* hungry,' a spokesman for the Kenyan government said, declining the gift.[3]

MONGOs wave criticism aside on the grounds that large, traditional aid organizations make mistakes too. Big mistakes. The European Commission once sent supplies of food aid to Africa that contained traces of radioactive contamination.

Other MONGOs fly themselves in, rather than supplies. On arrival they rent a car, stick a decal on it to identify their organization and they're in business. The only documents they need are tourist visas – and even those aren't required in countries where the central government is weak or has ceased to exist.

In his book *Giving: How Each of Us Can Change the World*, Bill Clinton writes of an 'explosion of private individuals who devote themselves to a good cause' and interprets this explosion as an 'unprecedented democratization of charity', attributing it to the fact that television and the internet have made us increasingly aware of the fate of people who suffer as a result of wars and natural disasters.[4] No one has any idea how many MONGOs currently exist, whether private initiatives, church projects, funds, foundations or associations. Tsunami territory was virtually crushed under the weight of spontaneous initiatives. Anyone typing 'tsunami' and 'donation' into Google in January 2005 had a choice of over 60,000 referrals to MONGO websites, the vast majority representing brand-new organizations.

In the Netherlands more than 16,000 charities have so far been registered, but this tells us nothing about the true figure, nor about the actual number of MONGOs working in disaster zones, since registration is not compulsory. Individual aid work is trendy nowadays in Great Britain, the Scandinavian countries and Australia. In the United States, the most generous country of all, the Internal Revenue Service grants tax exemption to an average of eighty-three new charities a day, and more than 150,000 have been registered so far.

When the money runs out, the MONGOs go home, but they rarely wind up their organizations, often choosing to remain in existence long after the suffering is over. MONGOs that sent convoys of supplies to orphanages in post-revolutionary Romania in 1989 popped up again in Bosnia in 1994–5. Some re-emerged in Darfur ten years later. Attempts have been made to look into the backgrounds of the MONGOs that arrived in Goma in 1994–5, and although much remains unclear, the details that have emerged suggest that many were established for good causes in Eastern Europe in 1989 and had no previous experience either of Africa or in the field of emergency relief.[5]

MONGOs can tell you nothing about the impact of their work, since they carry out no studies, says Dr Lau Schulpen of the Centre for International Development Issues (CIDIN) at the Radboud University in Nijmegen, the Netherlands. He has looked into the effectiveness of private initiatives in Ghana and Malawi and believes we ought not to take at face value the claim that they work more efficiently than established organizations. 'They account for themselves mainly through newsletters, which report on how specific individuals are getting along and who has spoken to whom, but fail to say what their activities have meant in practice for the target group.'[6]

★

MONGOs were active during the great Dutch flood disaster of 1953, when in heavy storms with force ten winds a number of dykes gave way. Hundreds of people spontaneously set out for the provinces of Zuid-Holland, Brabant and Zeeland. They wanted to help seal the dykes but succeeded only in adding to the chaos in the affected area. The Dutch VPRO television programme *Andere Tijden* (Other Times) conducted research into the disaster relief effort and concluded that the Dutch Red Cross and the army, attempting to coordinate relief, soon found they had no grip at all on private initiatives. On 4 February, three days after the dykes broke, the Red Cross broadcast a desperate plea: 'We urge everyone to stop collecting supplies right across the country until further notice.' Pile after pile of clothing had been donated and would need to be stored, sorted and distributed. Warehouses in The Hague were soon bursting at the seams. 'It was a serious hazard, too,' a warehouse worker said. 'If you have large stocks of clothing in one place, there may be a risk of infection. Not all of it was clean.'

But instead of easing off, the influx of goods increased, and supplies soon began arriving from abroad as well. Ships full of second-hand goods were unloaded at Rotterdam. Timber arrived from Finland, sugar from Jamaica, blankets from Sweden, 6,000 crates of oranges from Israel, 6,000 bars of Eau-de-Cologne scented soap from Germany, 12,000 kilos of knitting wool from America, rice from Iran, 1,000 kilos of dates from Iraq, and spectacle frames, torches, buckets, barbed wire, toys, candles, chocolate, sandbags, wheelbarrows and tractors from all over the world.

Both the Dutch Red Cross and its parent organization, the ICRC, learned a great deal from that flood. They never again put out a call to the public for donations of goods and supplies. 'The spectre of a mountain of tens of thousands of single shoes would always stay with them.'[7]

The world of do-it-yourself aid is deeply haunted by the spirit of the priests of yore. Religious MONGOs, especially those based in America, are the fastest-growing branch of the aid industry. In Afghanistan they distributed Bibles along with meals, until the Islamic Afghan government put a stop to it.

'In the plane from Nairobi to Khartoum I sat next to a bunch of American Christian hippies with guitars. They'd been given money by their church so that they could go and spend three weeks in Darfur bringing "hope",' a member of staff of a Norwegian NGO in Sudan told me in 2005.

In huts, in school buildings and on the village squares of other African countries in crisis, religious MONGOs are forever setting up 'born again' churches, while self-appointed prophets from the Pentecostal and Baptist churches of the American Bible Belt virtually trip over each other in West Africa in their efforts to contribute to the post-war moral revival of Liberia and Sierra Leone. So many of them wanted to hire the football stadium in Freetown that a waiting list developed; one 'travelling salvation show' after another was staged there, with believers dancing, singing and speaking in tongues. Their banners brightened streets blasted to rubble in the fighting: 'Experience Holy Lighting' in 'Super Natural Happenings' with 'On Stage Divine Healings' and 'Inexplicable Miracles', including resurrection from the dead. Such performances were not wasted on the local population. Religious to their hind teeth, they streamed into the stadium in their tens of thousands, several times a week if they could afford the entry price.

'Why bring evangelism to a country that's already a hundred per cent religious?' I asked one evangelist, Billy Bob, a sprightly fifty-something who had travelled to Africa all the way from Texas.

'Because Africans still don't understand that God disapproves of people bashing each other's brains in,' he answered with steadfast conviction.

The Mercy Ships, a small fleet of retired cruise liners converted into floating hospitals, owned by a religious leader from Texas, bring 'hope and healing' to war zones. I climb aboard a Mercy Ship that has docked in the harbour at Freetown. The First-Class Reception still sports gilt-edged doors and marble floors.

Only those who need simple surgery requiring little after-care – cataracts, squints or cleft lips, for example – are treated by the floating doctors. When patients wake from the anaesthetic the treatment continues: at every strategic spot in the recovery room a TV screen shows a film about the life of Jesus, over and over again. Dubbed into dozens of languages and dialects, from Urdu to Mandarin, *The Life of Jesus* is part of the standard baggage of evangelists all over the world. On board here today they're showing a version in the language of the Krio people, but when the doctors discover a Temne patient in one of the beds, they inexorably thrust a version with a soundtrack he can follow into the video machine.

'What we are doing, God would do too,' one of the surgeons believes. Some Muslim patients are converted even as they lie there, still hooked up to a drip, he adds.

The Islamic province of Aceh, in Indonesia, hit by a tsunami on top of a rebellion, was besieged by MONGOs bringing 'hope' and occasionally 'healing'. Along with mainstream Protestant and Catholic organizations, Mormon MONGOs sprang into action and the Church of Scientology sent volunteers in bright yellow T-shirts to apply mind-over-matter healing techniques to survivors. Dozens of Western doctors set off alone in hired Jeeps, past flooded villages, with first-aid kits on their back seats. Some residents of Aceh Province said they'd been examined three times, by three different doctors, none of whom had any idea what the previous one had said, done or prescribed. Many MONGO doctors did a good job, but several made incorrect diagnoses because they were not familiar with local diseases and parasites.

One MONGO that wandered through a refugee camp in Liberia in 2004 consisted of a group of American medical students, who carried out procedures they weren't licensed to perform in the US. Then there was Feed My Lambs International, which descended on the displaced of Sierra Leone.

The founder and director of this particular MONGO was Lonny Houk from Kansas, a retired health administrator with the Department of Defense. His mission: in the face of war, hunger or AIDS, to go wherever human suffering is chronic and do there what Jesus would have done. He's happy to tell his story. When he retired in 1995 he had everything he needed, except a purpose in life.

'Then I thought of Jesus. "Do you love me?" Jesus asked Peter. "Yes Lord," said Peter. "You know I love you." And Jesus said to him, "Feed my lambs."'

When Lonny Houk read in the newspaper about the war in Sierra Leone, he passed the hat around among family and friends and flew to Freetown. By the time I met him he was on his third visit. He proudly showed me a pile of clippings from the *Kansas City Star*, a six-part serial about an earlier mission of his.[8] It begins with a meeting at his kitchen table in a suburb of Kansas City, with Houk and some friends leaning over a collection of photos.

'*Look at this kid,*' *Lonny says, tossing a photograph to Dan*. '*They chopped him in the skull with a machete. You can see his brain move,*' wrote the *Kansas City Star*. Using a disposable camera from Wal-Mart, Houk had snapped photos of the wounds suffered by more than 200 people now living in refugee camps and villages, victims of the country's civil war.

'*Man, oh man, Lonny,*' *Dan says*. He picks up a magnifying glass and takes a closer look at the photograph of the hacked skull. Dan was on an earlier trip to Sierra Leone with Houk and he'll be on the next one too. *He considers medical missions a hobby, a way for him to confront 'the enormous frontier of poverty' around the world*. Tom, director of a Bible camp in Montana, will join them. So will Carl, an orthopaedic surgeon from Alabama; Marsha, his friend and a nurse at an elementary school, 'used to treating scraped knees and runny noses'; and Jan. Like Marsha, Jan has never been abroad before. Sarah, another nurse, is the seventh member of the team.

They travel on tourist visas. '*Leave your emotions behind,*' is Houk's final instruction before they take off. '*Don't think.*'

Operate, pray, eat, pray again, sleep, get up, pray, then operate

again, on dozens of people one after the other. The team has only
a week to spend in the country and they've yet to move on from
Freetown to Bo, behind the front line. There too people need
help.

I read on.

In a twenty-by-twenty room made available to the team by a
Sierra Leonean contact, a man with a gunshot wound and an
amputee sit on stretchers. Carl and Dan operate simultaneously.
They administer spinal anaesthetics. There's no electricity. No fresh
air. No water.

*'If there's no water,' Dan says, 'get one of those bottled waters in here and
we'll go with that,'* the paper continued.

'We need to check his blood pressure. Do you have a stethoscope?' asks Carl.

No. The team has forgotten to bring one. But the man with the
gunshot wound has already been cut open. Carl is probing the
wound with his fingers.

'Do it by pulse then.'

Bending over his patient, Dan suddenly sees a funny side to the
situation. *'Imagine! Some strange white guys run in [. . .] can't speak your
language, give you an anaesthetic. Us putting him on this stretcher must have
felt like an alien abduction.'*

He starts sawing off a piece of the patient with something that
resembles a gigli saw, a steel wire stretched taut between the two
prongs of a handle. The leg stump needs shortening. White bone
dust puffs into the air until finally the saw is through. A square piece
of bone with a chunk of flesh attached flies up into nurse Sarah's
mask and dances away across the floor.

'Any blood?' Dan wants to know. He was concerned about AIDS,
the article adds.

'A little speck on the mask,' Sarah answers. Dan takes a step back
to admire the reworked limb. *'That was good tibia, hard bone.'* He
looks closer. 'Hate to say this, but it should be shorter.'

Meanwhile, team leader Houk is hurrying through a crowded
refugee camp, 'assessing patients in seconds. But Lonny's on high-
speed, adrenaline-fueled automatic pilot.' Who will die if he's not

operated on immediately? Who can still live for a while without surgery? My astonishment mounts. The article fails to explain who or what qualifies a retired health administrator to make a diagnosis, let alone in a few seconds.   ·

In Bo, Sierra Leone's second city, a couple of hours' drive from Freetown, a series of operations is scheduled. Houk's team has set aside a day and a half for them. In part two of the newspaper series I read that after a virtually sleepless night the gigli saw is brought out again.

Exhaustion has begun to set in.

A mother produces her seven-day-old baby, begging the team to treat it. The child's legs are turned almost backwards; a congenital defect. This problem is simple to fix, Carl thinks. *'Dan remains uneasy about anaesthetizing a baby this young in primitive conditions. Jan has doubts, too. On the other hand, she feels desperate looking at the baby. Nobody's going to help this child unless we do something, she thinks. Nobody.'*

By the time they arrived, more than 300 INGOs were at work in Sierra Leone, including medical giants like MSF and the ICRC, but Houk's team had apparently managed not to run into any of them anywhere.

A couple of hours later the child was dead.

'I wonder about that operation,' Dan said. 'Should we have done one knee at a time? I think both knees was the way to go.' Marsha: 'The baby had no future. We offered it something.'

The mother of the dead child was waiting outside on a wooden bench under a mango tree. In America Houk's doctors might have been hauled before a medical disciplinary board, but here in Africa, I read, they paid for a bus ticket so that the mother could get back to her hut in the refugee camp, then lifted their next victim on to the operating table. Who says a human life can't be quantified in cash?

The publication of the newspaper serial has generated so much support for Houk from churchgoers in Kansas that he's thinking about expanding his rescue work to cover Darfur.

He waves away criticism when I ask him whether that's a good idea. 'It's perfectly simple. Aid work is something you just have to want and then do.'

After Houk's lightning visit, the American NGO World Hope, whose offices were a short distance from the US embassy in Freetown, found several of the post-operative patients lying bleeding in their doorway. The operations had been free, but proper aftercare turned out not to be part of the package. By the time stitches worked loose and infections burst open, Houk and his team were back in Kansas.

Reverend Santiagu Kanu of World Hope, who'd hired a nurse to stem the bleeding, was still angry when I visited him. 'Extreme recklessness,' he deemed it. 'Check a few stitches, they said, when they asked if we could do the after-care. But they left no money at all for it. We had to repeat some of the operations at our own expense.'

Just as a wheelchair user has a right to protection from helpful people who try to push him across the road against a red light, you'd think victims in war zones would have a right to protection from aid workers who arrive unannounced and set about their work without the most basic qualifications. But that right is not laid down anywhere. On the contrary, far from fending off amateurs, ministries for developmental cooperation and traditional aid organizations are increasingly willing to finance the projects MONGOs come up with. Annual and quarterly reports from major aid agencies often feature them as 'implementing partners' and 'local partners'. Large aid organizations encourage the trend towards do-it-yourself aid in order to boost public support for humanitarian aid as such, which indirectly benefits donors and traditional aid organizations. Failures go unreported, because criticism of MONGOs reflects badly on the aid industry in general, which comes under fire often enough as it is.

The authorities in the countries MONGOs visit are rarely well enough organized, especially in situations of crisis and war, even to ask the MONGOs that are flooding in exactly what they're coming to do. In 1995 the Rwandan Tutsi regime proved itself to be a positive exception. A year after the genocide it was organized enough to expel from the country fifty MONGOs that could offer no clear explanation of who they were and what they were doing.

4. Donor darlings

Someone complained to Voltaire that life was hard.
'Compared to what?' asked Voltaire.

The camp for Sierra Leone's amputees, people whose limbs had been hacked off by rebels and soldiers during the civil war, was in the middle of the capital, Freetown, right next to the busy two-lane road to the ocean. Murray Town Camp clung to the side of one of Freetown's overpopulated hills. In huts built out of thin tree trunks with UNHCR tarpaulins draped over them lived 226 amputees, some with a couple of close relatives, 560 people in total. From the pumps where they scrubbed their cooking pots, themselves and their children, a constant stream of soapy water seeped on to the road, and the steel fence around the camp was festooned with washing.

In front of the gate was a small forest of notice boards nailed to posts, bearing the logos of aid organizations: Médecins sans Frontières, CAUSE Canada, World Hope USA, UNICEF and several names I didn't know. In between the signs lounged bored camp-dwellers, some on crutches, others with shirt sleeves flapping empty, a few with ears or lips missing. Several were trying to sell UNHCR tarpaulins, still in their plastic packaging, to passers-by for the equivalent of €10. But most were just blankly watching a line of cars, trucks, *pudapudas* (battered minivans), poultry, stray dogs and pedestrians trail slowly past.

The view of the ocean far below was obscured by smoke from dozens of cooking fires. The occupants of the villas above the camp, which clung to the same hillside, would have preferred the amputees to leave sooner rather than later. One INGO had already offered to build a whole new neighbourhood for them at the edge of the city. There they'd get to live in real little houses, surrounded by patches of land for growing vegetables. Wheelchair users would be able to reach their front doors along specially tarmacked lanes. The tracks between the huts in Murray Town Camp were too narrow for that and the terrain too muddy and steep; amputees parked their wheelchairs on the road near the camp entrance and hobbled or crawled from there to their huts on the slope.

The camp was crowded, dirty and impractical for disabled people, but the amputees refused to leave – during the war for fear of rebel attacks on the suburbs and later, after peace came, because in Murray Town Camp it was easy for foreign journalists, donors and aid organizations to find them. Not that such visitors could steer clear of the camp even if they wanted to. The amputees were the icons of Sierra Leone's civil war. Of all the war victims in West Africa, foreign aid workers tried hardest to be associated with them.

'If we'd gotten hold of God, we'd have hacked His hands off too,' Sierra Leoneans said about what they'd done to each other. But that was with hindsight. An estimated 200,000 people were killed in the civil war (1991–2001), the majority of them civilians. In those eleven years of insanity, all parties to the conflict – government troops, rebels and pro-government militia – indulged in rape, looting, arson, killing and mutilation on an astonishing scale.

For the first few years the outside world knew little of what was going on. The violence took place mainly in the bush, which had little to recommend it to outsiders (other than a few diamond dealers) even before the war. Only when an increasing number of people emerged out of the bush with their hands, arms, feet, legs, tongues, lips or ears hacked off with machetes and axes was a UN resolution passed, followed up with intervention by the West African peacekeeping force ECOMOG.

'Long sleeve or short?' was the choice they'd frequently been offered when rebels stormed their villages: amputation at the shoulder or at the wrist. But usually people simply had to wait and see which bits of their bodies they'd lose.

Of the estimated 4,000 people who suffered non-medical amputations, at least half quickly died. They bled to death or succumbed to traumatic fever. An estimated 1,600 survived. According to Sierra Leoneans, who remained extremely devout despite everything, the survivors ought to be grateful to the Good Lord. But the peace-keepers of ECOMOG deserve a share of the credit. The mostly Nigerian troops who found amputees alive during their bush patrols sometimes had coagulants, iodine or even tetanus shots to give away. They loaded the agonized wretches into the backs of their pickups and drove them to the old, full-to-capacity hospital in Freetown. Several hundred amputees stayed in the city after their treatment was over, along with their families, because their villages were in rebel-held territory. It was for them that Murray Town Camp was built.

Like pit-bulls in a kindergarten, journalists from all over the world pounced on the story of the amputees. From CNN and the *New York Times* to Dutch public television and the *South China Post*, they all managed to find Murray Town Camp. Partly as a result of media attention, Sierra Leone became the beneficiary of the largest UN peace mission and – in terms of dollars per head of population – the largest humanitarian aid operation anywhere in the world at the time. Around 300 INGOs rushed to the little country. Even organizations that were not there specifically to help amputees used photos of people in Murray Town Camp in their fundraising campaigns.

'It's never been so easy to collect money as it is with the pictures of these poor devils,' said a member of staff at an INGO in Freetown.

On paper the local authorities were responsible for everything that went on in Murray Town Camp, but civil servants delegated the management of the camp to MSF France. That organization soon threw up its hands, since neither the camp-dwellers nor the aid workers, nor indeed government officials, were willing to respect MSF's authority. If the MSF manager said no to yet another new relief project or yet another camera team, there was always a minister, official, camp chairman or aid organization that could be moved to say yes, whether or not in return for a small gift.

'International interest in the amputees is greater than we had anticipated,' MSF France wrote to the Sierra Leonean Minister of Health in its letter of resignation. It described the 'endless parade' of people trying to capitalize on the publicity value of the amputees, 'including the amputees themselves'. National and international delegations came and went whenever it suited them and for whatever reason. Ministers swept potential donors off to visit the camp as a warm-up ahead of aid negotiations. INGOs that were not even working with amputees arranged tours of the camp for important contacts to underline the desperate needs of the Sierra Leonean people, while diplomats breezed in to be photographed displaying their sympathy.

MSF France also complained about the many 'individual philanthropists and associations, religious or not, who rope in local politicians in order to gain access to the camp with their – sometimes overlapping – projects, which often serve no purpose beyond taking photos and making films for their fundraising'.

The *pièce de résistance* for each and every tour of the camp was a little girl who had been only three months old when rebels hacked off her arm. For each foreign visitor the mother rolled up her daughter's sleeve. Like a professional child star, the toddler would pose with her naked stump thrust forward, her little face a picture of misery.

The endless stream of visitors meant that MSF France was unable to fulfil its task of 'protecting human dignity' in the camp. The organization declined to accept responsibility for the consequences. 'Even the amputees' recovery process is jeopardized by the sheer number of visitors,' it wrote.

Max Chevalier, a Dutch physiotherapist at Murray Town Camp who was medical coordinator and acting chief of mission for a French NGO called Handicap International (HI), echoed the experience of MSF France. 'Our intention is to enable amputees to return to a normal life. But that's not what they want. They'd rather stumble around dramatically without their prostheses. Donors love that and the photographers and TV camera teams pay them to do it,' he explained.

It's bad for children in particular to fail to wear their prostheses. 'If a child does as he's told and wears his prosthesis from a young age, he'll build the correct muscles. If not, the stump becomes soft and deformities develop. But photographers pay even the children to wave their bare stumps about.'

None of the other INGOs dared to take over MSF France's position as camp manager. So Murray Town Camp remained a humanitarian free-state, where everybody – press, politicians, aid workers and amputees – did whatever he or she liked.

Since it was every man for himself, a no-holds-barred battle for money and attention broke out between the amputees in the camp. For two years, until 2001, some 500 of them lived together as a unified group. Then one lot of camp-dwellers decided to separate from the rest. They called themselves the 'real' amputees: people who had been maimed by rebels. Those from whom they chose to distinguish themselves were people they called the 'war wounded', whose limbs had been amputated by doctors, perhaps because of gangrene resulting from gunshot wounds, or after rebels had tried but failed to chop off limbs because their axes or machetes were blunt. Their wounds had become infected, so eventually a doctor had to complete the amputation. The real amputees felt they had a greater entitlement to the donations that were pouring in. After all, it was thanks to campaigns based on their stories that the money had been made available.

Tensions between the real amputees and the war wounded came to a head after a visit to the camp by the president of Ghana, John Kufuor, in January 2001. Kufuor left a donation of $10,000 in cash. The real amputees refused to share the money with the others. A mass fight broke out and the real amputees thrashed the war wounded. 'Literally,' said Chevalier. 'They let fly at each other with crutches and prostheses and kicked and hit each other with their stumps.'

Beaten into retreat, from then on the war wounded lived beyond the limelight in Grafton Camp for the War Wounded on the edge of the city.

Murray Town Camp had been in existence for four years when I first walked in, but an average of three to four international delegations per day were still turning up at the gate. They always brought camera teams and photographers with them, so that their backers could see them making speeches and handing over money and supplies. For three days I tried to keep track of the visitors. First I noted the arrival of a certain Mrs Iki, director of an organization called Advocates for Human Development Toward Self-Reliance in Sierra Leone, a Japanese INGO, who burst into tears during her tour of the camp. With Japanese television cameras rolling, she promised several puzzled amputee onlookers that she would do her best to get help for them from Japan.

She'd only just left when a truck chartered by a Baptist church in the American state of Virginia pulled up with a large consignment of used clothing. A clergyman – people said he was called Sherman Brown – climbed out of the driver's cab and assured the amputees selling UNHCR tarpaulins at the gate that American churches sympathized with their lot and said he hoped they would all follow his example. He left the clothes in one great heap at the side of the road, encouraged the refugees to continue believing in God and left.

Next to show up was the leader of the Sierra Leonean United National People's Party, Dr John Karefa-Smart. He'd brought a small army of local journalists with him in his Land Cruiser. While cameras clicked, Dr Smart dragged five 25-kilo sacks of rice out of the boot of his vehicle.

'I am very much in sympathy with you,' he declared to his audience of camp residents. 'Although I am not as equal to you, my sympathy for you is that I am also an amputee; though small, it has disturbed my career as a doctor greatly.' He waved his right hand to the watching throng. The middle finger was missing.

The next morning I heard on the local radio station Kiss FM that the African Union, speaking from Addis Ababa, had promised to donate $250,000 to the amputees. At that very moment an aid agency based in Germany was delivering a container-load of second-hand toys to the gate.

That afternoon news began to circulate that a fundamentalist Muslim aid organization had arrived at Murray Town Camp. 'Hamas', a camp resident told me. Coincidence or not, later that afternoon a poster was suddenly pasted to the camp gate announcing an evangelical meeting for the amputees, to be held by an American group called Jesus Is Alive 2000.

The day after that, Dutch diplomat Peter van Walsum came to visit in his capacity as a delegate from the UN Security Council in New York. 'The Volendam of West Africa', he called Murray Town Camp, referring to a major tourist attraction in his home country. 'Visiting the amputees means being part of the circus, but if you don't visit them, people say you haven't really been to Sierra Leone.' He'd decided to come 'just briefly', to enter the camp for a minute or so and then leave again.

Max Chevalier too watched the endless stream of visitors forage around in the camp. 'Sometimes they'll send e-mails, saying they're on their way to Sierra Leone to give the amputees courses in embroidering serviettes, or pottery, but they've yet to find places for the teachers to stay and, oh yes, participants. Could we make the arrangements? Churches ring us to say they've sent shipments of second-hand clothing or food parcels, and they're sure we'd be willing to steer the deliveries through customs and distribute them in the camp. I drove into the camp one morning and found people I'd never seen before standing at the gate in white coats handing out antibiotics. Then they vanished. No idea who they were. Recently one of my patients died of an overdose of medication. It's a mystery to me where she got it.'

Chevalier's phone rang. A French journalist was about to come and film the amputees and wanted Chevalier to guide him around the camp.

'Now listen,' Chevalier said into the receiver. 'In this country three hundred and three out of every thousand children die before they reach the age of five, from malaria, diarrhoea and anaemia. Why not make a film about that?'

But no, they had to be amputees.

'I can't refuse to cooperate,' Chevalier told me. 'I don't have the right to deny the amputees media coverage.

'A truck drove up,' he continued his story. 'The ramp came down and heaps of prostheses rolled out on to the street, cast-offs from an American rehabilitation clinic. Those folk were amazed the amputees didn't throw themselves on the artificial legs, weeping with gratitude. But everybody here has plenty of prostheses. From us alone they've each received two. A cosmetic one, which gives a passable impression of a real hand or leg, for looks and for morale, and one that may not be particularly attractive but performs a function, an arm with a hook, for instance.'

Chevalier pointed to a pile of artificial limbs in a corner of the Handicap International workshop. 'Brought here by an agitated American woman. We don't need any of those, madam, I said as politely as I could. She was deeply affronted. "Are you the one to decide that blah blah!" Okay, I said. Just put them over there then.'

And 'there' the American feet, legs and arms still lay. In fact artificial limbs were lying around all over the camp, gifts from generous souls the world over, flung into tangled heaps in corners.

Prostheses were popular gifts and it was easy to raise funds for them. Two INGOs were already competing with Handicap International to become the main supplier of prostheses to Murray Town Camp. One organization, staffed by Vietnam veterans who had lost limbs themselves, set up a workshop where people could be fitted with artificial feet with splits in them, so that they could wear flip-flops. The American organization World Hope offered the same models as HI, only 'lighter, more comfortable and easier to repair', according to World Hope itself. To persuade amputees to wear World Hope prostheses, particularly when camera teams were in the camp, the programme coordinator tried giving away free wrist-watches with the artificial arms. Neither the arms nor the watches made it into the news and World Hope curtailed its promotional initiative.

But the latest, and according to Chevalier the most disturbing, marketing ploy in the camp was to drop the idea of bringing aid to the amputees like everyone else and instead take the amputees to the aid.

'Almost all my child patients have already been taken out of the camp by aid groups no one's ever heard of. Look.' Chevalier pointed to his forearm: goose bumps. 'I get those every time I talk about it.'

It started in September 2000. 'Something was brewing in the camp. The patients were whispering about "going to America". I asked around, but no one would tell me what was up. One amputee blurted out, "If I say anything, I won't be allowed to go." There was an air of extreme secrecy,' Chevalier said.

'Then the director of the Coca-Cola factory in Freetown rang me. He had five amputees in his employ; none of the five had arrived for work that morning. Did I know what was going on? Jalloh, the night watchman at the Handicap International office, who had lost both his hands to the rebels, had failed to turn up for work too. Later I gathered that as many as thirty amputees had left the previous day on the ferry to Conakry in neighbouring Guinea. They were hanging around at the American embassy, because they'd heard rumours that amputees were going to be given visas for America.'

That same week an American man reported to Chevalier, saying he was acting as a contact for a group in New York called Gift of Limbs. He confirmed that some amputees would be allowed to go to America, but they had to be minors.

'Gift of Limbs is going to save these children,' the man told Chevalier. He proudly showed him six brand-new passports for child amputees. All six were among Chevalier's patients.

Chevalier asked him why the children needed to go to America.

'They'll get prostheses there,' the American answered.

'They already have prostheses,' Chevalier told him.

The American seemed surprised at first, then suspicious. 'The children say they don't,' he said.

'The children always tell foreigners they don't have prostheses – and that no one's looking after them and they haven't had a bite to eat for weeks,' Chevalier sneered. 'They know better than to tell you they're already receiving help, because then you won't give them anything. But go and take a look inside the huts,' he advised. 'Then you'll see their prostheses. I know you will, because we made them for the children ourselves! It's just that they don't wear them when white people are around.

'And besides,' Chevalier went on, into his stride now, 'you must have noticed that all those kids have a shape.' A 'shape' is a surgically formed stump over which an artificial limb can be fitted.

At first the American looked at Chevalier dumbfounded, but he quickly recovered. 'The prostheses we're going to make for them in America are better than anything you can manufacture here. State of the art. The latest high tech.'

Chevalier tried to explain to the man that post-amputation treatment takes years. Children who are still growing must have their stumps measured every six months and their prostheses adjusted. Further amputations may be needed, since a child's bones will continue to grow, right through the skin. Treatment has to go on until a child is fully grown.

'"If the children are given high-tech prostheses, they won't be able to get follow-up care in Sierra Leone. No one can do anything high tech here. Sierra Leonean manufacturers of artificial limbs have neither the expertise nor the materials for advanced techniques. Or are you going to come and fetch those kids every six months for a follow-up in America?" I asked,' Chevalier continued. 'But the fellow didn't know anything, except the time of the flight to the States. He'd made all the preparations in the deepest secrecy and nothing could stand in the way of the children's departure now.

When I continued to protest he said: "You're jealous, because we're going to give them something you can't give them."'

Six days after that first contact with Gift of Limbs, it was discovered that the selected children, aged between four and fifteen, had left.

'Gift of Limbs didn't even ask me for their medical records. Those children had all sorts of problems besides missing arms. That was the simplest thing to treat. They were severely traumatized; they'd lost family members, some had been raped. It's all in their files. I rang and offered to send the paperwork on to New York, but they never responded,' Chevalier told me.

Weeks later an American colleague faxed him a copy of a *New York Times* article. 'The children had been met at the airport in New York by a battery of TV cameras and a weeping Democrat senator, who proudly declared that he'd acted as a mediator during the process of getting visas for them. I realized it was almost election time in America.'

After Gift of Limbs came a man called Sam Simpson. His organization, based in the American Bible Belt, took three amputee children: Fatmata, one of Chevalier's patients in Murray Town Camp, and two from Grafton Camp for the War Wounded.

'And again it was all done with extreme stealth,' Chevalier said.

Sam Simpson had seen a photograph of Fatmata in an American newspaper. The story described how, at the age of eleven, she'd fallen into the clutches of rebels. They'd hacked off both her arms.

'I immediately travelled to Sierra Leone to look for her,' Simpson told me. When I met him in Freetown he was already on his third visit to the country.

'At last I found her. She was sitting under the big cotton tree in the centre of town holding out her little stumps, begging. I stopped my car next to her and said: "You will suffer no more. You're coming with me to America."'

I asked Simpson why the girl needed to go to America.

'She didn't have any prostheses,' he answered. 'All those rich aid organizations in this country and no one had done a thing for her.'

I consulted Chevalier, who was the aid coordinator responsible for Fatmata at the time.

'She certainly did have prostheses,' he said. 'Two. We'd made them for her ourselves, but she was a vain teenager. She thought they were ugly and hid them.'

I went back to Simpson. 'Well, all right, she did have one of those with a hook, but she thought it was hideous. Scandalous, isn't it? So many rich NGOs in this country and all they can come up with is one of those cheap hooks.'

Simpson took Fatmata's friend Sophia, twelve years old at the time, along with them to America.

'They were sitting there under that cotton tree begging together. Sophia had a terrible infection in her arm. Rebels had tried to hack it off and given up halfway. In Freetown they weren't doing anything for her. All those rich aid workers are far too busy holding meetings about their danger allowances and per diems. The child was sitting there with a filthy stinking bandage around her arm.'

'I don't know Sophia. She was living in Grafton Camp,' Chevalier told me. 'But what I do know is that if Simpson had spent the money it cost him to fly those two girls to America on treatments here instead, he could have relieved dozens of children of their supposedly filthy stinking bandages.'

Simpson saw the matter differently. 'If all the hundreds of rich NGOs wandering around here picking their noses took a couple of kids home, they could help every single child in Sierra Leone,' he scoffed.

Simpson hadn't asked for Fatmata's medical records. 'There weren't any records,' he insisted. 'Nobody in this country has medical records.'

'Poppycock!' said Chevalier. 'The existence of medical records and doctors assigned to individual patients simply doesn't fit with the story a man like that tells in the Bible Belt to raise funds for his little NGO!'

Back in the US, Simpson had adopted the girls. They'd already featured in the national weeklies twice, in the local papers a dozen times, and they'd appeared as guests on a whole range of television programmes. Sometimes they were invited to speak three times in one day.

'I say yes to those requests as often as possible,' Simpson said. 'Africa must be helped and my girls are instrumental in that. A lot of fat lazy Americans are jolted awake when they see my girls' poor little arms.'

Sometimes Fatmata and Sophia didn't feel like performing for the umpteenth time. 'But they're aware of their responsibility and they live up to it. They know I didn't take them out of Sierra Leone for nothing,' said Simpson proudly.

'In America fat lazy people have to be jolted awake and he needs to keep himself awake too. That was his aim in taking those girls away from here,' Chevalier snarled. 'It's got nothing to do with medical need and everything to do with him feeling good about himself and raising money for his precious little NGO!'

After Fatmata had been taken to America, Chevalier marched off angrily to the Ministry of Social Welfare, Gender and Children's Affairs in Freetown, which had signed the papers giving permission for the children to make the trip.

'I told the minister they couldn't go letting children leave for America without their families. To which she replied: "Oh, those kids had been uprooted anyhow." Then she threw me out of her office.'

The six children who'd left for New York with Gift of Limbs back in 2000 had been no less in demand there than Fatmata and Sophia were in the southern States. Soon after their arrival in New York they appeared as special guests at demonstrations on the steps of Tiffany's against giving 'blood diamonds' as Christmas presents. They'd been on *Like It Is*, a programme about African-American

affairs on WABC-TV, and they'd addressed the General Assembly
of the United Nations in New York and the Congressional Africa
Committee in Washington. On that occasion the *Washington Post*
wrote:

> The six children arrived in Washington in late September, malnourished
> and withdrawn, with stumps where arms and legs had been. [. . .] Today
> they are different, and they don't want to go back. The children are
> said to be romping about downtown Brooklyn with their prosthetic
> arms and legs, noticeably heavier in new name-brand jeans, jackets
> and sneakers donated to them. [. . .] They eat as much as they want –
> from spaghetti to ice cream – live in a comfortable hotel on Staten
> Island and get informal schooling, physical therapy, counseling and
> weekly swim time at a YMCA.[1]

'I say no,' the reporter recorded ten-year-old Fatu as saying when
she was asked whether she wanted to go home. 'I love here, I don't
love Sierra Leone any longer.'

Shortly before the visas for the children in New York were due
to expire, Carmine DeSantis, president of Gift of Limbs, declared
that the children would not be allowed to return. 'They're not going
back – at least not for now – and we're going to do everything in
our power to do right by them,' he told newsmen. He had retained
a lawyer to file asylum applications for the amputees. The Gift of
Limbs phone was ringing off the hook with people who wanted to
take the children into their homes, he said. Little Maminatu, four
years old and with only one arm, was deployed in the publicity
offensive for asylum. The *New York Times* photographed her sitting
on Bill Clinton's lap during a celebrity fundraiser picnic with 1,000
guests on Staten Island. 'You've given them a lot more than limbs,'
Clinton told the organizers.

'When these children were still living in Africa, they had two
wishes,' a picnicking supporter of Gift of Limbs added. 'One to go
to heaven. The other to go to the United States.' Joe Mandarino,
co-founder with DeSantis of Gift of Limbs, added: 'Our plans are

to get this whole group situated, to get the children adopted and in good homes.'

The Rotary Clubs of Staten Island and Brooklyn covered the costs of the children's stay. They said they were convinced the children couldn't possibly return to Sierra Leone, since their lives would be in danger there. The threat came not just from rebels but from other amputees in Murray Town Camp who, so they'd been informed, had no prostheses or only cruder models and might target the children for their nice new limbs, their American clothes and the toys they'd been given.

'Besides, even if the children survived the envy of others, there's no infrastructure in Freetown to repair the prosthetics or to adjust them for the children if they grow. It's like taking a Mercedes and trying to run it in the jungle.'

'Duh!' exclaimed Max Chevalier when he reached that point in the *Washington Post* article.

'Adoption?' Confused, Maminatu's father studied the back of the photo of his little girl sitting on Clinton's lap, as if hoping he might find something written there that he could actually read. He was illiterate. We were sitting in Murray Town Camp on empty Fanta crates outside his plastic hut. 'Gift of Limbs seeks American adoptive parents for the children. It's in the newspaper,' I nodded.

I asked him if he'd signed anything giving his consent to adoption. He thought for a moment and remembered at some point having put a cross under something. The ministry had told him he must, otherwise Maminatu wouldn't be allowed to go to America. Other parents had put their crosses to documents too, but they hadn't been given copies. They'd get those later, the official had said.

Fatmata's father, also living in Murray Town Camp, became similarly confused when I asked him about the papers signing her over for adoption by Sam Simpson. He too had put a cross to something at some point. Other than that he knew only that Fatmata had new American arms. He'd been sent a copy of an article from an American newspaper. He kept it in a plastic shopping bag hanging from a coat-peg. Next to it, on a bent nail, was the prosthesis with the hook that Fatmata had never wanted to wear. In one newspaper photo his daughter looked radiant as she watched a white man clasp a silver armband around her artificial wrist. Fatmata's new arms were battery-powered, the caption said. She'd already written 'Ilovegodjesus' with them.

Fatmata's father received a quick phone call from her every few months. She would ring the office of a church in the neighbour-hood.

'When she gets new parents, where are her mother and I supposed to go?' he asked me. 'You can only stay here if you're an amputee or looking after an amputee. I'll tell Fatmata that next time.'

Sophia's mother, living in Grafton Camp for the War Wounded, had also put a cross to a piece of paper. A white man had taken Sophia with him. She'd asked him if he was a doctor and he'd said yes.

'Her child was taken too,' said a neighbour as I stepped out of Sophia's mother's hut. The neighbour pointed to a young woman in an old, faded yellow dress. While I'd been inside, a circle of people had formed outside the door.

Mohamed Sesay was the name of the woman's son and he'd been six years old when white people took him away. During the war the rebels had hacked the child's head. 'It looked like this,' said the neighbour. He pulled a girl of about seven into the circle. Her head was bald. Her skull bore the scars of deep gashes. I asked Mohamed's mother who had taken her son. She didn't know. 'The camp chairman wrote down the name of the man, but he's lost the piece of paper,' she said, shrugging.

But I knew who'd got Mohamed: Sam Simpson had 'brought him home'. That was what he called it when he took children back with him to America: 'bringing them home'.

People said it was a miracle Mohamed had survived the blows to his head, but Simpson knew the boy was alive for a reason. 'God wanted me to find him,' he said. Mohamed's head wounds were such that it was dangerous to expose him to the pressure fluctuations involved in air travel. 'But how could I go home and say to people: I came across a little boy with holes in his skull and did nothing?'

Mohamed survived the journey.

The people thronging around me were starting to get restless. A rumour had spread that a white woman was in Grafton Camp to fetch children. People pushed and pulled children through the crowd and pressed them to me.

'Take this one with you,' somebody hissed. 'No, this one!' others called out. 'This one!'

Back in Murray Town Camp I heard from Chevalier that two more of his young patients had disappeared. 'Someone saw them in the departure lounge at the airport, two small children without arms accompanied by a white man with a moustache. They were waiting for a flight to Abidjan. Someone asked him who he was. The fellow answered that he was a doctor and he was on his way to America to treat the children.'

'The children are not at death's door, and the fact that children are poor is no excuse for taking them away from their parents. Millions of children in the world are poor.' I'd asked the UNICEF spokeswoman in Freetown, Roisin De Burca, whether it amounted to child stealing if minors were taken from Murray Town Camp. She wasn't completely sure. 'It's forced separation in any case. The children can go with them to the land of milk and honey, but they have to leave their parents, brothers and sisters behind.' She added that 80 per cent of the children in Sierra Leone are not registered anywhere, so they're an easy target for trafficking.

I then went to see the American ambassador in Freetown, Joe Melrose, and asked him why the US had given the children visas. With his untrimmed hair and stubbly cheeks, Melrose looked to me like a cross between a Colombian drug dealer and the film-maker Michael Moore. He explained that all visas for Sierra Leoneans were issued by the American embassy in neighbouring Guinea. 'I only do the pre-screening in Freetown, for the medical cases among the visa applicants. I look at the files, if there are any that is, otherwise I just look at photos of the children. If I conclude that their wounds can't be treated here, then it's a case of medical need and I recommend to Guinea that the request should be granted.'

'With the children in Murray Town Camp there was no question of medical need, was there?' I asked.

'True,' said Melrose.

'So why did you recommend they should be granted visas?'

'For political reasons,' he answered. 'Amputee children have been politicized. One example: recently I had some member of Congress or other on the phone from Washington again, arrogantly demanding I tell him what the fuck was the problem with the visas for a group of amputee children. Pretty remarkable, since those visas hadn't even been applied for yet. Get the picture?'

'Are you afraid of headlines in the paper: "Melrose Refuses Visas for Amputee Children! Does He Want Them to Die?"'

'Sure I am,' said Melrose.

'Are you worried about the fate of those children in America?'

'Hell, yeah!' he said.

'Children grow fast once they get to the US. After they've been de-wormed they explode! Fatmata and Sophia both wear bras already,' Simpson told me. The girls were doing well in America, but bringing them up wasn't always easy.

'At first they had minor disagreements. Fatmata said she had a right to more pocket money and nicer clothes because Dad, that's me, had gone looking for her and had come upon Sophia only by chance. Then Sophia would get angry and try to scratch Fatmata's eyes out and Fatmata would knock Sophia to the ground with her stumps.'

Fatmata is a spoilt brat, Simpson is the first to admit.

'What do you expect? She used to be one of the sweetest amputees of all, eleven years old when the rebels got hold of her. Every photographer, every camera team in Murray Town Camp has immortalized her. Everyone gave her everything she wanted, sweets, attention, money, because she was so terribly cute and so heart-breakingly maimed.'

Fatmata had also earned good money begging in the centre of Freetown, Simpson heard later. The better the girls learned to speak English, the more he got to know about their lives.

So now if Fatmata wanted something and didn't get her way she would lose her temper and snarl at Simpson that he ought to have left her in Sierra Leone, because she'd had her own money there and could do whatever she liked.

'All right, sweetheart, I say. I'll buy you a ticket today. Just pack your suitcase. Then she backs down.'

She regularly did little cleaning jobs for the local minister and earned $5 a time. She hadn't spent a cent. 'She's very good at getting other people to pay for her,' said Simpson. 'She's saving. She wants to build a house one day for her Sierra Leonean parents.'

There's a lot of pressure on the girls to send money and gifts to their families, he tells me. 'I try to steer that in the right direction, or even to let the contact fizzle out. I get my informants in Murray Town Camp and Grafton Camp to check what their parents are up to. Listen, sweethearts, I say, the way your parents hold out their hands to you just isn't right. Your mothers are pregnant yet again! Yes, but that was actually a good thing, Fatmata said, because an eighteen-month-old sister had just died. That's right, I said, she's under a pile of stones in Murray Town Camp. I've had a photo taken of the grave. That sister died because your mother didn't care for her properly. We bought her a foam-rubber mattress so that she and the baby had somewhere dry to lie down in the hut, remember? And she sold it. So now the baby's dead. Yes, but, Fatmata said, my mother wants a dress. The last time we sent her a dress she sold that too, sweetheart, remember? Those people will never get anywhere if they go on like that, I tell her.'

Simpson is quiet for a moment. Then he spits: 'That camp should be closed down and the people sent back to their villages! Now that their amputees aren't around to profit from they should look after themselves. Let them grow bananas and shoot monkeys! But they can't be bothered. They stay there for free, get their rations twice a week and ask their daughters to send dollars and dresses. And what does that Fatmata do? She tapes messages for her parents! Saying things like: "I'll never be able to enjoy all the things I have now, because I know you're suffering."'

Around the same time, a website providing information to humanitarian aid organizations featured a flashing appeal for donors by a German NGO. It urgently needed to cover the cost of tickets to Germany for twenty-five Sierra Leonean amputee children, who were to be given life-saving medical treatment in Germany. Christ End Time Movement International was the name of the organization.

'Gift of Limbs, Christ End Time . . . You can rely on the occupational sector itself to think up the creepiest names imaginable for aid organizations,' Chevalier shuddered.

The twenty-five children had already been selected, the organization wrote.

'There go the last of the minors in the camp,' Chevalier said when I told him. 'I'll start flushing their medical records down the toilet then.'

'The big aid money circulates among Western organizations. At least let our children be *ours*!' I'd tracked down the boss of the Christ End Time Movement International in Freetown. He turned out to be Douglas Mead, director of the Road Transport Company, Sierra Leone's public transport service. If things continued to go well with the Christ End Time Movement International, he would give up his job and go to live with the children in Germany, he told me.

The country's public transport system had been shut down for four months by the time I spoke to Mead, since he hadn't paid his staff in all that time. People said no one dared try to get Mead to toe the line because on his mother's side he was a first cousin to Sierra Leone's president, 'Pa' Kabbah.

Mead had set up the Christ End Time Movement along with a

cousin who'd been living in Berlin for thirty years. The original aim of the movement had been to cultivate religious awareness among the German people. 'But it turned out we couldn't get donors for that. Now that we've dedicated ourselves to helping child amputees, money is starting to come in.'

He licked his lips and leaned towards me. 'When we saw what all those American organizations were doing with the amputee children, my cousin and I thought: We can do the same thing. And better!'

The two cousins decided to squeeze the American organizations out of the market in a single move by laying claim to twenty-five children. For a start, anyhow. In their project proposal for donors they asked for \$1.5 million per year for a hundred amputee children. While the cousin in Berlin looked for a building to house them all, Mead went to Murray Town Camp with an official from the Ministry of Social Welfare, Gender and Children's Affairs to 'earmark' all the amputee children they could find for his Christ End Time Movement.

'These twenty-five can't be taken by anyone but us. The youngest is five. Really cute.'

I asked him what selection criteria they'd used.

'The children had to be amputees and no older than eighteen,' he answered.

'Other organizations have never heard of the Christ End Time Movement,' I ventured.

'Nor I of them,' Mead replied breezily. 'No idea who all those foreigners are who've managed to get access to Murray Town Camp. We deal with our government, not with foreign NGOs.'

'Why is it medically necessary for the children to travel to Berlin?'

'They'll be given prostheses there.'

'They have those already.'

'Maybe. But ours will be better.'

'Won't they miss their families?'

'No, they're all orphans.'

'What does Christ End Time actually mean?' I asked when I got to the door.

'I wondered that too,' said Mead. 'It's translated from the German. The meaning got lost in the process.'

I decided to visit the minister responsible, Shirley Gbujama, of Social Welfare, Gender and Children's Affairs.

'The children call me Auntie Shirley. So nice. They even ring me up in the middle of the night: "Auntie! How are you, Auntie?" To thank me for letting them go to America.'

I'd found Mrs Gbujama at her ministry, sporting a T-shirt with an advert for an anti-malaria programme and a matching cap. She'd just got back from an NGO promotional party and she'd brought her second-in-command, Theresa Vamboi, along for the interview. 'Acting Chief Social Development Officer, also responsible for Sierra Leone's child protection,' Vamboi introduced herself.

'The children all come back to Sierra Leone after their medical treatment.' Gbujama was certain of that.

'Really? Gift of Limbs has hired a lawyer to put the children through the asylum process,' I said.

'It depends how you define asylum,' Gbujama attempted to reassure me. 'Asylum as in "fled"? That wouldn't make any sense. The children had my permission to leave, so how can they have fled? Asylum as in "extension of stay for medical treatment"? That's possible perhaps.'

'They're looking for adoptive parents for the children, but Maminatu's father, for example, wants his daughter back,' I said.

'Surely not?!' Confused, Gbujama leafed through a pile of paperwork on the desk in front of her. 'Maminatu . . . Mami . . . But her father signed her over for adoption, didn't he? Theresa? Check that out!'

Theresa Vamboi leaned back and gestured dismissively. 'The man's lying. He didn't want the child any more. He'd told his wife to run away if the rebels came and she didn't. So when the mother was killed and the child suffered amputation he decided it wasn't his problem.'

The minister: 'All the same, the documents have to be in order, Theresa. Otherwise we'll be in trouble. Go and look for the release form!'

'Later,' mumbled Vamboi, sluggishly wafting away a fly in mid-air.

'How many travel permits have you issued for children so far?'

Gbujama: 'Six.'

Vamboi: 'Eight.'

Gbujama: 'Eight? Let me think . . . Gift of Limbs has four, I believe.'

'Six,' said Vamboi.

'And Sam Simpson has three,' I said.

Gbujama: 'Sam Simpson? Do I know him, Theresa?'

Vamboi: 'Yes.'

Gbujama: 'Why aren't those children in my files then?'

Vamboi: 'Because before they left for America all three were adopted by a Sierra Leonean. Ministerial permission for the trip wasn't necessary after that.'

'Which Sierra Leonean adopted them, then?' the minister asked crossly.

'Your cousin, George.'

I knew this George. He was a local partner of Simpson's. When I met him he'd bragged about his excellent relations with the minister. 'Auntie Shirley even spanked my bottom when I was a child,' he said proudly.

'I hope that was all, darling. It's twelve-thirty already,' the minister said, getting up.

'One more question,' I replied quickly. The minister already had her hand on the door handle. 'Don't you think the Christ End Time Movement is intending to take an awful lot of children?'

'How many? Theresa?'

Vamboi: 'Twenty-five.'

The minister: 'So many?'

'It's all legal. We helped them with the selection,' said Vamboi.

The minister: 'Really? What was there to select, then? An amputee is an amputee. Or not?' Suddenly she'd had enough of me. 'You make it sound as if we're the enemies of those children! That Max Chevalier must have sent you, right? He's just jealous. He wants to keep all the children for himself.'

Vamboi nodded: 'Jealousy, yes. Everyone wants to earn money with those children.'

Lamin Jusu Jarka was the chairman of Murray Town Camp. Before the rebels caught him and hacked off both his arms he'd been head of security for Barclays Bank in Freetown. Vice-chairman of the camp was Gibril Sesay, who'd lost his arms and ears in the war. In 1978 Sesay had been a midfielder in Sierra Leone's national football team. I asked them whether they knew anything about foreigners taking children.

'Sure!' they answered in unison. 'Every week two or three foreigners come to the camp asking questions about children. Whether they have parents, whether they're hungry.'

The chairman and the vice-chairman never asked the foreigners who they were, or why they wanted to know such things. They didn't speak to all of them in person by any means. 'Not all white people know that the camp has a chairman and that he's the person you're supposed to ask questions like that. A lot of them just talk to anyone they come across in the camp.'

Recently Sesay had spoken to the uncle of sixteen-year-old Mariatu. An American and an Englishman had been in touch, saying they wanted to take the girl away for medical treatment.

'A beautiful girl, fair in complexion,' Sesay said.

'Without arms,' Jarka nodded.

'One of the men is called Larry and the other one's tall, dresses in military clothing and has a scar on his top lip,' said Sesay.

'The uncle wanted our advice,' said Jarka.

'We told him he should ask the white men for a lot of money,' said Sesay.

'Ask for money? But those two men want to help the girl, don't they?' I feigned utter astonishment.

Jarka and Sesay looked straight through me, saying nothing.

After a long pause Sesay broke the silence. 'What do you think of my ears?' He'd been given two new ears that morning by foreigners. Lovely cosmetic ones.

'What I need,' said shopkeeper Abu, 'is a child.' I always bought my beer at his kiosk in town. I asked him what he needed a child for.

'To fetch water for me, to sweep the floor and sleep in the shop to chase away thieves,' he replied. 'Tomorrow I'm going to get myself a nice one.'

I didn't really want to know, but I asked anyway: 'Where are you going to get a child like that?'

'In Murray Town Camp,' he answered. 'You give the chairman some money. You promise to send the child to school and then you can take one with you.'

'Do you wanna come to America with me?' Sam Simpson once asked a child who had suffered severe burns. The little boy had never been out of his village, didn't know what a light switch was and couldn't understand how you could get to the upper floor of a house. Simpson slapped his thighs at the memory.

'You ready to go?' With a little pile of clothes on his head, the child had pitter-pattered faithfully behind Simpson to his pickup. Cheered by his friends as he left, he'd ridden off towards his new future.

Once in America the boy proved unmanageable. He was placed in two different foster homes, but in no time at all they simply wanted to see the back of him.

'Stick him on a plane; we don't care if the old crate makes it all the way to Africa or not, just as long as he's on it,' they told Simpson.

'So I said to that child: you're going back to Africa! And the kid said: "No! No! In Africa I die!! I stay here!" So I said: no, you don't belong here. You're an unbelievably annoying child and you belong at home in a palm tree picking coconuts and you should be thrashed twenty times a day. Because that's what the boy needed, discipline. That was impossible in America. Can you imagine, giving a burnt little Sierra Leonean war victim a good hiding?'

In the departure lounge at the airport, an action group – Simpson called them 'do-goodies' – had made a final attempt to prevent the child's departure. He was crying heartrendingly. But Simpson persisted, even though people told him he was mean and cruel.

We'd called in on the little boy's Sierra Leonean family that morning. An uncle was convinced the reason the child had behaved so badly in America was that he was bewitched. He promised to take him to an exorcist if Simpson was willing to fly the boy back to America afterwards. Simpson had answered that nobody in America would ever want to look after the child.

On our way to the car for the drive back to Freetown, Simpson turned his attention to a little girl in the bunch of children that was following us, giggling. He said exactly what he'd said to the boy with the burns: 'You wanna come to America with me?'

The little girl gave a high-pitched scream and fled to her mother's skirts, peering out from behind them, eyes wide with terror, to check Simpson wasn't coming after her. To my horror the mother didn't say, 'Come to Mummy, it was only a joke.' Instead she pushed the child back towards Simpson. He picked up the little girl, grabbed her hand and flapped it up and down.

'Say bye-bye! Bye-bye! I'm going to America!' he cooed in a babyish voice.

'Bye-bye,' went everyone around us, including the mother. I looked at the child and saw the expression on her face turn from deathly fear to resignation to her fate.

'Bye-bye!' she waved. At that point Simpson put her back down on the ground and roared with laughter: 'Joke!'

The whole village humoured him by laughing along.

★

October 2006. The children who travelled to New York with Gift of Limbs have lost none of the pulling power they had when they were first taken out of Murray Town Camp. Plump and in the peak of health, a Sierra Leonean girl called Damba appears on television, sitting on a sofa next to Oprah Winfrey. Damba was nine years old when, together with her mother, Fina, she suffered amputation – short sleeve; one whole arm each.

In her hut in Murray Town Camp, with Damba's youngest brother at her breast, Fina had shown me photos taken on the day Damba left with Gift of Limbs, wearing her prettiest dress, snow-white with lace frills. In one of the photos she was being hugged by a white woman. Fina didn't know who the woman was, but she'd believed her when she assured Fina that in America Jesus would give her daughter a new arm. A few weeks after Damba's departure, a photo arrived in the post showing her sitting on Santa Claus's lap. The envelope also contained a $100 bill. Since then, Fina said, she had heard nothing more.

Damba, sixteen years old now, has never been back to Sierra Leone. Adopted by an American couple, she attends high school. Oprah wants to know whether she still sometimes thinks about her Sierra Leonean mother.

'Yes,' says Damba.

Well, then Oprah has a surprise! 'Your Sierra Leonean mother is here.'

Oprah's audience jumps up out of its seats, cheering, crying and applauding. Fina shuffles into view from the wings. She's wearing a new dress and has her prosthesis on, I notice, but how thin and bent she looks among all those gigantic Americans, her daughter included.

Oprah says that her team has managed to get a visa for her mother for a few weeks. When those few weeks are over, Fina will have to return to her mud hut in Murray Town Camp.

Monrovia, 17 May 2007, IRIN:

Orphanages are big businesses in Liberia attracting millions of dollars
in international assistance every year, yet 80 percent of the so-called
orphans living there are not parentless at all, according to Liberian
government officials and child rights activists. 'Most of the children
living in almost all of the orphanages in this country are not actual
orphans, but have been used by orphanage owners to seek external
funding for their personal gains,' Vivian Cherue, Liberia's deputy health
minister for social welfare, who is responsible for regulating orphanages,
told IRIN.

Furthermore, many orphanages are 'sub-standard' according to a
report issued in March by the Human Rights and Protection Section of
the United Nations Mission in Liberia (UNMIL). In 11 out of Liberia's
15 counties, orphanages constitute 'major human rights problems', the
UNMIL report said.

The number of orphanages in Liberia has mushroomed, from just 10
in 1989 to more than 120 today, according to information provided by
Liberia's health minister.

Orphanage owners block efforts to re-integrate children into their
families and even snatch children, various experts told IRIN.

In October that same year a French aid organization called
L'Arche de Zoé (a variation on Noah's Ark) turned up at an
airport in Chad. It was founded in the aftermath of the tsunami
to provide 'aid to orphans'. Zoé was an Indonesian girl who
had survived the tsunami. After the orphans in the tsunami
zone had been rescued, the organization extended its area of
operations to the African desert. The Chad police arrested six
of its staff and three French journalists travelling with them at
the airport. A chartered Boeing was already warming up to fly
103 children from Chad and Sudan to France. Founder Eric
Breteau, a fireman and one-time chairman of the French four-
wheel-drive federation, declared that for the children, all of
them orphans, the journey was 'medically necessary'.

The organization's website is fiercely critical of 'the international community that is doing nothing to stop the bloodbath in Darfur'. L'Arche de Zoé wanted to save children from the hell of the camps there. 'We will no doubt provoke the wrath of all sorts of politicians, philosophers and other "great thinkers", who will cry scandal and speak of ethics, illegality or the psychological traumas of uprooted children,' the site predicts. 'But isn't the extermination going on in Darfur scandalous, illegal and traumatizing?'

The cost of the operation was estimated at €550,000, including €165,000 to charter the Boeing. Some of the money came from the 300 French foster families who'd been lined up to care for the children for at least five years.

'These aren't sick, starving and abandoned creatures in the desert. In the local context these are healthy, well-nourished children,' a spokesman for the UNHCR in Chad declared on television.

UNICEF had spoken with the children and reached the conclusion that many did not come from refugee camps and were not even orphans. 'According to the name they gave, they all come from a village near the border between Chad and Darfur. A number of them told us their parents were still alive and they'd been lured away from their village with sweets and biscuits,' a UNICEF spokesman said.

Then came footage shot by a cameraman who had travelled with the French rescuers. It shows bandages soaked in iodine being applied to children who have nothing wrong with them. 'There, now you look like a real war victim,' a French lady chuckles.

5. Aid as a weapon of war

*We have local customs authorities who want to squeeze out money
from our relief supplies. We have guerrilla leaders and paramilitaries
and generals and government people who basically don't care if
people die as long as their prestige is massaged.*

Jan Egeland, UN Undersecretary-General for Humanitarian Affairs
and Emergency Relief Coordinator (2003–7), on one of the challenges
facing humanitarian aid workers in war zones[1]

On the main road outside the capital, Monrovia, the Liberian rebel
movement LURD had set up roadblocks every few kilometres. It
was 2002. As we approached each nail-spiked plank on the tarmac,
I wound down the car window a little and hurriedly threw out a
white unsliced loaf. I was then waved through. I kept a supply of
bread on the back seat. The rebels were always hungry. They were
still growing.

Negotiations for access to war zones are often dressed up in rather
more ritual. At every village he needed to pass in one piece, a UN
employee travelling through rebel-held territory in West Africa
would politely ask to speak to the chief. 'The guards at the village
boundary always tell me I'll have to wait, and they point to a tree-
stump. I install myself on it. For a long time nothing happens. Then
somebody comes out of a hut with a chair on his head, followed by
someone with a table. From other huts women emerge with cooking
pots and firewood, even a fan. They turn the path into a compound,
quite pleasant really. And then, once the rice is boiling, the man
himself finally arrives. His boys stride ahead of him with their
Kalashnikovs, to shove children and goats off the sandy path. He
settles down on the chair, which has been placed next to the pot of
rice. He looks in all directions except mine. He strokes his belly
lovingly and leaves the negotiations to his deputy. The toll varies.

I've come upon chiefs who let me through in return for a ballpoint. It's also happened that I've failed to get away with anything less than the promise of a shopping trip to the capital for the chief's wife, in a UN helicopter.'

No access to war zones without payment, whatever form it may take. Especially if you're a humanitarian. Warlords try to siphon off as large a proportion of the value of aid supplies as they can. During negotiations with INGOs in Liberia, the then president, Charles Taylor, demanded 15 per cent of the value of aid, to be paid to him in cash.[2] The Liberian war victims weren't the only ones who had to eat, after all. Taylor's troops did too. In Somalia the entrance fee charged by warlords ran to as much as 80 per cent of the amount the aid supplies were worth. And, according to the head of the UN mission in southern Afghanistan, Talatbek Masadykov, in 2006 aid organizations in Uruzgan handed over one-third of their food aid and agricultural support to the Taliban.

Estimates suggest that Indonesian soldiers walked off with at least 30 per cent of tsunami relief for Aceh Province – 30 per cent is also the average slice of the Indonesian military regime's state budget that 'disappears' annually. Soon after the tsunami, the people of Aceh saw soldiers selling sacks of donated rice to local traders, and there was a torrent of reports about aid supplies disappearing even before they'd been fully unloaded at the airport in Banda Aceh. Alwi Shihab, Indonesia's most senior official for disaster coordination, dismissed reports of people in Aceh Province suffering from hunger as a result of this kind of theft. 'I guarantee you no one's going hungry here apart from me. I haven't had lunch yet today.'

From the proceeds of their negotiations with INGOs, warring factions feed and arm themselves and buy support. Irrespective of the consequences for the length and ferocity of wars, INGOs and MONGOs – and indeed journalists – are free to make agreements, pacts, contracts and deals at their own discretion with wannabe presidents, tribal chiefs, warlords, troublemakers, rebel leaders, headmen, insurgents, terrorist cells, child generals, splinter-group kingpins, militia leaders, bosses of factions, transnational terrorist commanders, regime bigwigs, mercenaries, freedom fighters and underworld figures reincarnated as paramilitaries, at village, regional or national level. 'Humanitarian territories' in war zones are free markets where anyone can set out his aid stall, as long as he can agree terms with local power-brokers. Striking bargains with parties to conflicts is sometimes referred to as 'shaking hands with the devil'.

There are no rules and no limits, and no requirement to have any understanding of the local balance of power or to coordinate with other parties involved, humanitarian agencies included. In fact, for reasons of competition and PR, aid agencies often choose not to discuss details with their fellow organizations.

Aid agencies intending to set up projects for victims in, for example, Somaliland and Puntland, regions that have seceded from Somalia, may be faced with the demands of some five self-appointed rival presidents and a dozen prime ministers, all out for each other's blood. At any moment more may be added: in the never-ending peace negotiations in Nairobi there are peak days when no fewer than sixty presidential candidates participate. Attempts by a UN humanitarian representative to find somebody in Somaliland with the authority to negotiate terms for aid provision degenerated at one stage into a heated meeting with forty-eight of the area's 'generals', each of whom laid down conditions of his own. 'They begrudged each other the light of day, let alone any credit for the clinics and water installations we were offering to build.'

You may be in serious trouble if you refuse to listen to two-bit generals like these. In eastern Congo the powerful leaders of the Hema people decided to permit the arrival of international aid organizations only if they agreed to give their enemies, the Lendus, nothing – despite the fact that the Lendus were demonstrably in more acute need. In 2001 six ICRC workers who did help the Lendus were murdered, and in response to threats MSF suspended its work in the region.

In war-torn northern Sri Lanka, reconstruction after the tsunami was impossible without negotiating with the rebel movement, the Tamil Tigers. The Dutch arm of Caritas built emergency accommodation in Tiger territory. 'We paid up to 25 per cent extra. All that money went to the Tigers,' the Dutch foreman of the project said. Every time Caritas delivered a cargo of building materials to the region, the Tigers charged import tax. All supplies had to be transferred to the Tigers' own trucks, which were driven by Tiger drivers, and the builders hired by Caritas had to pay income tax to the Tigers and buy all their sand from one particular place. The owner of the sand quarry had close ties with the Tigers. 'You find yourself in a kind of mafia situation,' the foreman said.

Many Western countries put the Tigers on their list of terrorist groups, and human rights experts called it a 'fascist organization' that ignored just about all human rights. Caritas decided such matters were outside its bailiwick and went on negotiating, unperturbed. 'We wanted to help the people affected; that was our aim. We didn't worry too much about the fact that it meant financing the Tigers.'

Caritas didn't need to worry about how much it was spending, either, since in the wake of the tsunami the charitable foundation raised millions of euros in Dutch churches. 'Then you're not swayed by 10 per cent either way.'[3]

In former Yugoslavia the UNHCR surrendered 30 per cent of the total value of its aid supplies to Serb armed forces. On the orders of the Republika Srpska, aid convoys on their way from Croatia to the ravaged villages and towns of Bosnia were detained at Serb roadblocks. Every time a convoy was stopped it was stripped of yet more of its load by hungry soldiers and militias.[4]

Once inside a war zone, it's essential to have a blind spot for matters of ethics. Warlords and regimes deluge INGOs with taxes, often invented on the spot: import duties on aid supplies, fees for visas and work permits, harbour and airport taxes, income taxes, road taxes and permits for cars and trucks. The proceeds go straight into their war chests. Chiefs and generals often demand to be compensated for the use made by aid organizations of water from village pumps. There are even taxes for the 'use' by INGOs of children for vaccination and casualties for rehabilitation.

Exchange rates applied to the foreign currency in humanitarians' pockets are another goldmine. During the aid operation for the Kurds of northern Iraq, for example, humanitarian departments of the UN were required to conduct all transactions in local currency at the official exchange rate, thereby helping Saddam Hussein's regime to earn $250 million in 1992 alone.[5]

Wherever aid organizations appear, local political, military and business leaders suddenly start driving around in expensive cars and building splendid houses. Prices in 'humanitarian territories' go through the roof; rents are the first to rise, since aid organizations are always in urgent need of an apparently unlimited number of square metres of living and office space, as well as warehousing for aid supplies. In the blasted ruins of Kabul, rents rose to levels higher than Manhattan after the humanitarians landed: for $5,000 a month a foreigner could have a tiny, abandoned hovel to call his or her own for a while. The buildings were mostly owned by rich Afghans living abroad. According to real estate agents, the landlords were usually Taliban or Northern Alliance commanders living in Pakistan and using their rental income to train militias.[6]

In war zones there's no chance of fair competition, since after a peace accord is signed it takes years for law and order to be restored. Constitutions have to be written, elections have to be organized, and warlords and army commanders hold on to power, having transformed themselves into members of the highest post-war business and political circles, with whom INGOs negotiate. So most of the houses and services INGOs need are provided by local war elites. Cousins, uncles and close friends of those in power have the best chance of being chosen to supply goods to INGOs and to run the restaurants and clubs where the foreigners spend their evenings. Providers of cheaper goods and services suffer intimidation, to deter them from taking part in the tendering process.

In 2002, two years after the aid circus rolled in, the clique that had governed Sierra Leone both during and after the civil war had yet to appoint an official responsible for agricultural development, but it had set up a ministry charged purely with the task of 'supervising' INGO projects and collecting import duties on aid supplies.

The day I came to visit the INGO minister, the lift in the Youji government building wasn't working. 'Our Dear Lord is punishing us,' a woman in a colourful robe gasped on the third-floor staircase. I knew better: not God but Sierra Leone's Senegalese fuel supplier had become fed up with them. The company in Dakar wanted its overdue bills paid and had suspended deliveries. The money had been pocketed by Sierra Leone's rulers; ships carrying diesel stayed away and the city's generators fell silent one by one. Computers, traffic lights, lifts: nothing was working. Civil servants slogged up the stairs in the dark, wheezing. I followed them, to the sixth floor.

Still pouring with sweat, I found the minister's secretary in a tiny office crammed with a solid but empty oak desk and a monumental three-person sofa with ornately carved legs. I had to climb over the arm to sit down, sticking my legs under the desk. The secretary and I were sitting knee to knee.

'Visitor, sah!' the woman shouted at the closed door behind her.

'What do they want?' I heard the minister's voice through the door.

'There's just the one and she wants an interview,' the secretary called back.

'Say I'm sick and have to rest. Say it's malaria.'

'He's got malaria,' the secretary turned to me. The minister wasn't going to waste his time. He wanted aid projects, not conversations.

In Sierra Leone, ministers were currently earning a salary of $350 a month and civil servants $50–$80. In countries like Sudan and Afghanistan the amounts are roughly the same. A little shopping plus rent and school fees and the monthly salaries of local government elites are used up. Even the president of Sierra Leone couldn't possibly live on an honestly earned salary alone: he was on the payroll for a little over $700 a month, his vice-president for $400.

So when an aid convoy rolls into town, contract fever strikes. Local governors promptly leave off governing. 'All our policy-makers do is strategize on how to get more aid money,' complained the Kenya-based director of the Inter Region Economic Network, an African think-tank.

The big handsome hero of a hugely popular Nigerian soap shown on television all over West Africa isn't a pilot or a fireman but a project leader for UNICEF. In every scene, the broad-shouldered hunk parades about in yet another dazzling outfit and beautiful women squirm at his feet. A civil servant or local chief attached to an INGO project as an adviser or supervisor can earn a salary dozens of times higher than normal. When the aid circus arrives, officials quickly turn all their energy and attention to the search for opportunities to attach themselves to INGOs, or to extend their association with existing projects. Local administrators can easily 'supervise' multiple, even competing, projects simultaneously.

The relevance, quality and results of aid projects are not a priority. 'The things local officials weigh up are: will they get access to imported aid supplies, training, study trips, per diems and people needing to rent houses and vehicles? Will an aid project put them in a position to hand out jobs to brothers and cousins? Does the road a donor wants to finance run past the minister's native village, or can they wangle a road-surfacing contract for an uncle? If the answer is no, then it may take a very long time to get the necessary permits,' a coordinator for the European Commission in West Africa explained to me. The story I'd just told him about a wheelchair project in Liberia had made him feel even more dispirited than he already was. Medical INGOs had arranged for a batch of wheelchairs to be flown in, to ease the sufferings of local war invalids. The chairs turned up in the streets of Monrovia modified into ice-cream carts and mobile shops. Vendors who had nothing wrong with their legs were using the chairs, while amputees and cripples went on dragging themselves on their hands and knees through the filthy streets. Local government workers had distributed the wheelchairs among their own kith and kin, who in turn had rented them out to small-time entrepreneurs.

A policy to combat theft and abuse could be implemented only if one INGO held a monopoly in a given district, village or country. With their own business interests in mind, however, aid organizations do all in their power to prevent exactly that outcome. MSF and Action contre la Faim saw no reason to refuse an invitation from the RUF, the Sierra Leonean rebel organization, to provide relief in RUF territory. Other INGOs were not welcome there, since they'd banded together to try to do something about the theft of aid by the RUF. The two 'collaborators' defended themselves by saying, in effect: We couldn't just let people in RUF territory die, could we?[7]

During much of the Cold War only a handful of aid organizations would descend on a conflict zone, so it was easier to present a united front against abuse. Gradually both more and more aid organizations and more and more donors have begun to compete with each other. Nowadays, if the World Bank says no to a proposed project, then an Islamic financier will say yes, and if Europe doesn't respond quickly enough, China will already have offered its services.

The recipients of aid have become adept at exploiting rivalry within the aid industry. Experience has taught them that manipulation of aid channels will not be punished and that even under-performing or pointless projects can have their funding renewed. Money has been assigned and it has to be spent. 'Even if we have an amount left over, the donors don't want it back. They want you to spend it and write an attractive report,' the head of the international aid department of the Dutch Red Cross told me.

Aid organizations and donors usually prefer to keep silent about the aid to war-torn countries that is extorted or stolen, and there's no collaborative attempt to quantify the damage. 'Reliable empirical evidence of the degree to which humanitarian assistance is diverted is often lacking, even though such knowledge may be fundamental to understanding the impact of the assistance [. . .] in potentially providing warring factions with additional resources,' wrote the Organisation for Economic Co-operation and Development, of which all important donor countries are members, in 1999.

MSF Holland, one of the many dozens of international aid organizations at work during the 2008 conflict in Chad and Darfur, did provide some empirical evidence. Staff at the MSF Operational Centre Amsterdam (OCA) calculated the total value of assets looted and fees paid to the governments of Chad and the Sudan (which are two of the many parties to the fighting). Of MSF Holland's budget for Chad that year (more than €3.5 million) 2.84 per cent was stolen or extorted and of the budget for Darfur (over €2.7 million) 4.47 per cent. 'While neither the proportion nor the total sums are shocking, the contribution to the war economy is nonetheless substantial,' writes MSF OCA. 'It must also be considered that the total resources either looted or paid to the two governments in taxes, visas and fees by NGOs, UN agencies and the ICRC would be much larger, particularly given that many of these are resource-heavy operations, including food and non-food item delivery.' In fact, the humanitarian operation in Darfur was the largest and most expensive in the world in 2008. At the start of the year, the costs for the coming twelve months were estimated by the UN at $825 million. The operation in Chad in 2008 actually cost even more than that, since not only humanitarian but military contingents were sent.

The MSF report goes on: 'It is also important to note that, although only the financial value of assets has been calculated here, vehicles and communications equipment have a value beyond their monetary worth for armed actors, increasing their capacity to wage war.' It concludes:

We are unable to determine whether our aid helps or hinders one or more parties to the conflict. [. . .] However, it is clear that the losses – particularly looted assets – constitute a serious barrier to the efficient and effective provision of assistance, and can contribute to the war economy. This raises a serious challenge for the humanitarian community: can humanitarians be accused of fuelling or prolonging the conflict in these two countries?[8]

The serious challenge remains just that. Perpetrators of abuse continue to escape punishment and aid organizations keep on coming, in increasing numbers, and with increasingly diverse forms of aid. Given the escalating frequency of donor conferences, it's clear they intend to go on like this for many years to come.

The growing number of aid organizations and the rising value of the aid supplies and services they deliver to warring countries make humanitarian aid an increasingly important supplement to war chests. The number of organizations and the amount of money they come to spend in countries with no other sources of income turn the aid industry, supposedly neutral and unbiased, into a potentially lethal force the belligerents need to enlist.

6. Refugee warriors

In the early days of the crisis in Goma, in the spring of 1994, a representative of the UN refugee organization UNHCR looked down from the slopes of the Nyarangongo volcano at the motley array of Hutu militiamen, soldiers and fleeing civilians on the plain at his feet and said: 'We've never seen anything like this.'

Ambassador Aldo Ajello, representing the European Commission in Goma at the time, also expressed dismay: 'We were confronted with a situation which was completely abnormal: the coexistence in the UNHCR camps of civilian refugees and military forces.'

The UNHCR endorsed this view in an evaluation report published in 2002: the explosion of violence in the camps and the corruption that resulted 'threw up a new factor for which the UNHCR was unprepared'.

The EC and the UNHCR, respectively one of the largest donors to the rescue operation in Goma and the largest aid organization on the ground, were demonstrating extraordinarily selective institutional memories with their 'unprecedented's and '*jamais vu*'s. Nothing about events in Goma was new or abnormal to humanitarians and their donors. At least it shouldn't have been. Fighters who conceal themselves among displaced civilians are employing a common military tactic. They are known in the literature as 'refugee warriors'. They've been an aspect of humanitarian practice ever since international aid to refugees began, but because the relevant conclusions have not been drawn, ways of operating have not been adjusted accordingly. Humanitarians help. Without asking themselves – aloud, anyhow – who exactly their clients are.

In international law a refugee is a person who 'owing to a well-founded fear of being persecuted for reasons of race, religion, nationality, membership of a particular social group, or political opinion, is outside the country of his nationality'. The same set of rules defines refugee camps, and indeed camps for displaced persons in their own countries, as 'safe havens', where civilians caught up in a war and forced to flee their homes can stay to await the outcome. So much for the theory. In reality many refugee camps are anything but neutral humanitarian havens. Some estimates suggest that 15–20 per cent of people living in refugee camps worldwide are refugee warriors, prosecuting their wars in between meals and medical treatments in the camps.

All over the world, refugee camps act as a magnet to warriors. Strategic withdrawal to a camp allows armies and militias on the losing side to avoid getting minced. In a refugee camp they have time to regroup, civilians to hold hostage as human shields against attacks, and a chance to recuperate. Rich international aid organizations provide food, clean drinking water, medical care, shelter, education and welfare, both for the fleeing troops themselves and for their families and supporters. It costs the fighters nothing, and supplies will be brought to the camps from thousands of kilometres away if necessary. By forcing fellow camp-dwellers and INGOs to pay 'taxes' and 'protection money', they can top up their war chests at the same time.

Since aid organizations have neither the power nor the resources to prevent abuse, they ignore or keep quiet about the problem. The UNHCR, the largest refugee aid organization, makes only very occasional reference to the phenomenon of refugee warriors on its website, and even then only as a responsibility of international politics.

The supply and distribution of drinking water, food and medicines – and control over them within the camps – is to a great degree contracted out by the UNHCR to 500 or more national and international NGOs, which goes some way to explaining why these organizations are no less discreet than the UNHCR itself about the refugee warriors. Like the UNHCR, dependent as it is on voluntary contributions from donor governments, NGOs and

INGOs can't afford to lose contracts because bad 'news' has got out about the presence of refugee warriors in camps.

International refugee relief organizations were faced with their first refugee warriors over half a century ago: the Palestinians. After the Arab–Israeli War of 1948–9, UN member states set up the United Nations Relief and Works Agency (UNRWA) to provide relief to hundreds of thousands of Arab refugees from what had been Palestine. The UNRWA camps that sprang up in Lebanon, Syria, Jordan, the West Bank and the Gaza Strip have since developed into fully fledged city states from which the 'freedom struggle' against Israel – and against each other – continues to this day. The recruitment of fresh blood is effortless in the camps; one uprooted generation after another has been trained to fight. When Sabra and Shatila, Palestinian camps on Lebanese territory, were attacked by Phalangist militia units in 1982, half the world was incensed, saying the militia had massacred innocent people, while the other half believed the attack was justified because the camps were in fact military bases.

In the 1950s more refugee warriors emerged, this time in Algerian camps for Sahrawi refugees from disputed Western Sahara. Supplied by the World Food Programme and other agencies, they first fought a war against the Spanish colonial government and then, after Morocco annexed Western Sahara in 1975, against the Moroccan government. Their movement is called the Polisario Front.

From refugee camps in eastern Sudan in the 1980s, Eritrean and Ugandan warriors took up arms against their respective fatherlands. From camps in Ethiopia the Sudanese rebels of the SPLA fought the Sudanese government. The rebels referred to the refugees as 'aid bait', used to lure humanitarian aid. In his book *What Is the What*, Dave Eggers tells the story of a former inhabitant of such a camp:

We were used for war, we were used to garner food and the sympathy of the humanitarian-aid organizations. Just a few miles away from our civilian camp, the Sudan's People Liberation Army (SPLA) had their own base, where they trained and planned, and there was a steady pipeline of supplies and recruits that travelled between the two camps. [. . .] While the humanitarian world fed us, the SPLA were tracking each of us, waiting until we were ripe. They would take those who were old enough, those who were strong and fit and angry enough. Those boys would trek over the hill to Bonga, the training camp, and that was the last we would see of them.[1]

In the mid-1980s, INGOs built a camp called Kakuma in northern Kenya. It was intended as a place of safety for fleeing Sudanese, but over the years refugees from war-torn Ethiopia, Burundi, Rwanda, Congo, Eritrea and Liberia have taken shelter there, with a peak of as many as 300,000 people in the 1990s.

The SPLA travelled to Kakuma along with the Sudanese refugees. As the number of aid organizations in the camp grew, providing new facilities and launching more programmes every month, SPLA influence within it grew too. Until sundown the camp was dedicated to UN programmes. People went to INGO schools and ate WFP rations. But after sundown the camp belonged to the SPLA, which came to take its share of the food from the refugees.

Kakuma became a kind of department store for the rebels. Commanders and soldiers 'shopped' there, not just for recruits but for eligible young brides.

Officially there was no SPLA presence at the camp, but former and current commanders moved through without check. [. . .] The camp was a militarized place, with rigid rules and far more intimations that we were there for one primary purpose: to be fed and fattened such that we might fight once we were large enough to do so.[2]

Many SPLA members installed their families in the camp.

The INGOs in Kakuma carried on undeterred. To this day, dozens of national and international NGOs run youth programmes, care for orphans, and offer creative therapies, trauma treatment and vocational training. One Japanese NGO disseminates culture in the form of drama groups, debating societies, art clubs and a camp library. Another Japanese NGO teaches refugees how to build and maintain websites. Through an NGO called Right to Play, the Dutch Olympic Committee organizes sporting activities for the refugees in Kakuma, while the International Rescue Committee (IRC) runs a project called FilmAid: entertainment and guidance through the medium of film.

Again in the 1980s, the Khmer Rouge found a safe haven in camps along the Thai border after the Vietnamese invasion of Cambodia. Accommodating 360,000 people between them, the refugee camps had courtrooms, gambling dens, pharmacies, Buddhist temples, a prison and a red-light district. The UN estimates that the Khmer Rouge managed to get its hands on 50–80 per cent of all the food aid and pharmaceuticals provided.

At the same time, Taliban fighters were being nurtured in UNHCR camps in Pakistan. The budding refugee warriors received food and medical care from INGOs, while the US government supplied them with weapons so they could fight Russian troops in Afghanistan.

The ANC guerrilla army, having entrenched itself among refugees in camps in southern Africa, was likewise provided with food and munitions, in their case to fight apartheid in South Africa.

SWAPO used refugee camps in Angola as bases for its operations. Refugee camps for El Salvadorians and Nicaraguans in Honduras received military supplies from Central American guerrilla movements. Fighters from Chad bivouacked among refugees in camps in Libya. Somali warlords sowed death and destruction from camps in northern Kenya. All were helped by INGOs.

The Tutsis who invaded Rwanda in 1994 and drove the Hutus out of the country to become refugee warriors in Goma were refugee fighters themselves. They had fled Rwanda in the late 1950s and were given refugee status abroad, with its accompanying package of rights and provisions. Their children returned to their fatherland in 1994 as a well-trained army.

The refugee enclaves in former Yugoslavia accommodated refugee warriors too. In Srebrenica, for instance, some estimates suggest that the number of Muslim fighters among the 15,000 Bosnian Muslim civilians was a good 2,000. From within the enclave they attacked Serb communities in the surrounding district.

In 1999 200,000 East Timorese fled to refugee camps in West Timor, which were supplied by INGOs but controlled by the East Timorese militiamen, policemen and soldiers who had fled along with them.

In Sierra Leone, again in the late 1990s, the Liberian refugees in UNHCR camps often metamorphosed into rebels after a few months. 'They come here only to rest up before going back to continue fighting,' complained frightened residents of areas near the camps. Today Turkish Kurds are still fighting Turkey from refugee camps in Iraq and Iran, and the Karen people fight the military dictatorship in Burma from camps in the Burmese jungle, cared for by humanitarians.

The presence of INGOs, often in large numbers, helps to foster the illusion of safety in camps and enclaves in war zones, even though the hundreds of millions of euros INGOs spend on them only help to make the camps more attractive to dangerous refugee warriors.

When international aid to refugees began after the Second World War, it was assumed that the international refugee problem would be all about individuals. Instead it was a matter of groups and entire peoples. The assumption was that it would be all about people escaping political persecution. Instead they were fleeing violence. Protecting refugees was presumed to be a judicial issue. In reality people turned out to need physical protection against soldiers and militias in and around the camps. Humanitarianism has no answer to any of this. Humanitarians build and supply refugee camps and enclaves but have neither the power nor the resources to keep armed warriors out of their clinics and food distribution centres.

It eventually made the Bosnians furious. After Bosnia declared independence in 1992, Serb nationalists went to war against them. Paramilitaries burned non-Serb villages to the ground and besieged several districts and towns, which the UN promptly declared to be 'safe havens'. INGOs prevented the people living in the enclaves from starving, but that didn't stop them being slaughtered by sniper fire and mortars.

'We have no need of you,' Bosnians yelled at the international humanitarians in the presence of journalists. 'We need arms to defend ourselves. Your food aid and medicines only allow us to die in good health.'

INGO staff themselves sometimes referred to their work in the enclaves as 'passing out sandwiches at the gates of Auschwitz'.

Sergio Vieira de Mello, who as Head of Civil Affairs of the United Nations Protection Force was involved in the UN operation for the besieged enclaves, called the humanitarian deliveries a 'frustrating palliative' for the Bosnians. 'You would get up in Sarajevo during that fucking winter and look at yourself in the mirror and wonder whether we were not the wardens of a huge concentration camp.'[3]

But he voiced that thought only after the war in Bosnia was over.

7. The hunger weapon

We came, we fed them, they got strong, they kicked our asses.

An American army officer during the strategic withdrawal of the US army from Somalia in 1995, on one of the dangers of distributing food aid to the enemy

'War is not carried on by arms alone. It is lawful to starve the hostile belligerent [. . .] so that it leads to the speedier subjection of the enemy.' So runs Article 17 of *Instructions for the Government of Armies of the United States in the Field*, 1863, known as the Lieber Code. Not until after the Second World War, in 1949, was the use of starvation as a weapon of war forbidden under the Geneva Conventions. Protocol 2, Article 14 states:

It is prohibited to attack, destroy, remove or render useless, for that purpose, objects indispensable to the survival of the civilian population, such as foodstuffs, agricultural areas for the production of foodstuffs, crops, livestock, drinking water installations and supplies, and irrigation works.

But those who wage war, be they Sudanese, Kosovars, Somalis, Afghans or Americans, nevertheless use the hunger weapon if they get the chance. It's quick, effective and cheap – and there are no sanctions for failing to comply with the Geneva Conventions.

If all goes well, then once famine has been inflicted on the enemy it gets even better: humanitarian aid arrives and the perpetrators help themselves. Armies, rebels and militias steal food supplies from warehouses or from international aid convoys and either consume them or sell them to top up their war chests. On balance, bringing food aid to a war zone can amount to a form of arms delivery.

★

'Think of the children in Biafra!' If you were small in the late 1960s, that was what your mother said to you if you didn't finish what was on your plate. The famine in Biafra was the first the Western world could follow on television.

Not since the liberation of the Nazi concentration camps had anyone in the West seen children looking like that, with the faces of little old men and bellies so swollen they seemed about to explode. What the viewers were not shown in the harrowing television coverage was that the famine had been caused and deliberately sustained by a jumped-up Biafran army commander using supplies of food aid intended for the victims in an attempt to win a war.

Biafra was one of Nigeria's most oil-rich provinces. At a glitzy champagne party on 30 May 1967, the provincial governor, Colonel Ojukwu, proclaimed Biafra an independent republic and appointed himself president. He garnered hardly any political support from abroad. Only Gabon, Ivory Coast, Tanzania, Zambia and Papa Doc Duvalier in Haiti recognized the new country. Militarily too, Ojukwu's position was hopeless. He was in command of 40,000 men, whereas the Nigerian government of President Gowon, who angrily decided to seize back the province, had an army of 180,000. Only the support of private humanitarian organizations made it possible for Ojukwu to keep his doomed little republic in being for a year and a half.

In September 1966 Ojukwu had appealed to the Ibo people, who were living all across Nigeria, to 'come home' to Biafra, where they traditionally formed a majority. He claimed that ethnic hatred outside Biafra was such that the lives of the Ibos were no longer safe.

The Nigerian authorities reacted to the declaration of independence by imposing a total blockade. Roads to Biafra were cut by the government army and bridges were blown. It became impossible to bring in food supplies. It was also forbidden. Hundreds of thousands of Ibos had 'returned home' over previous months. With them to feed as well, Biafran farmers could not step up production sufficiently to compensate for the food shortages caused by the blockade. Hunger set in.

Ojukwu was defeated militarily in the blink of an eye. In early 1968 the Nigerian army recaptured the Biafran towns of Calabar and Port Harcourt, which meant that Ojukwu had lost his airport, his most important harbour and his oil installations. He succeeded in using income from humanitarian aid to make up for the drop in revenue. In June 1968 he called in the Genevan PR company Markpress to mobilize world opinion in his favour with photographs and television images of starving children. The thrust of the publicity campaign was that the starving-out of the Biafrans was part of an attempted genocide against the Ibo people by the Nigerian government. The fact that despite their mass migration to Biafra, 7 million Ibos were still living all across Nigeria occurred to only a handful of Nigeria experts.

At the level of international diplomacy, negotiations took place with the Nigerian government to have food aid exempted from the blockade against Biafra, but most aid agencies decided not to await the outcome. A number of American religious organizations in particular set to work without delay, for 'the Biafran cause'.

With the roads blocked and no harbour or airport, the only connection between Biafra and the rest of the world was a stretch of road near a settlement called Uli that was just long enough to land transport planes. They came in at night, when it would be hard for the Nigerian army to shoot down aircraft heading for Biafra.

At first Ojukwu refused to allow the humanitarians to bring their own planes. They were forced to buy space for their food and medicines aboard Ojukwu's own veteran prop-driven aircraft. The rest of the hold was routinely filled with weapons and ammunition, so aid organizations were contributing to the expansion of Ojukwu's war arsenal. Ojukwu's army ate from the same food supplies, but because the humanitarians believed the relief of human suffering had to take priority, they told themselves it was permissible, indeed essential, to ignore the context.

Spaces in the hold that were left, between the munitions and the milk powder, were taken by international journalists invited by Markpress to come and report on the 'genocide'. British journalist

Frederick Forsyth, who later achieved worldwide fame with his
novel *The Day of the Jackal*, was among them. Western newspaper
readers and television viewers 'who couldn't fathom the political
complexities of the war could easily grasp the wrong in a picture
of a child dying of starvation', Forsyth said later about the fundraising impact of images from Biafra.[1]

In the summer of 1968 the Nigerian government allowed itself
to be mollified. Aid flights to Biafra could go ahead. There would
be no shooting at ICRC planes as long as they made use of a
specially opened air corridor. A few weeks later permission was
withdrawn again: Ojukwu was using the corridor to fly in arms.

Dozens of international organizations, including UNICEF,
Oxfam, Caritas, WFP, UNDP, the World Council of Churches
(WCC) and the Young Men's Christian Association (YMCA)
carried on with their illegal night-time deliveries. They each made
separate deals with Ojukwu about the fees they were to pay him
for the privilege. Even when aid organizations were allowed to
fly into Biafra in planes other than Ojukwu's ancient crates, he
continued to demand space on board for his munitions. He also
imposed exorbitant landing and import taxes on the humanitarians
for their aid flights. In dollars, cash. His international arms dealers
would accept only hard currency. Ojukwu set the exchange rate.
It probably made him a multi-millionaire.

The more supplies he received from international aid organizations, the less inclined the Biafran leader was to make any attempt
to end the sufferings of the Biafran people. While INGOs worked
their fingers to the bone trying to keep as many Biafrans alive as
possible, Ojukwu calmly devoted himself to designing and producing postage stamps and banknotes for his republic.[2]

Nearly two years and perhaps 2 million deaths later, most from
starvation, the game was up for Ojukwu. As Nigerian government
troops advanced further into Biafra, supplies of food aid to Uli
increasingly had to make way for supplies of arms. As a result,
Ojukwu's men had plenty of ammunition in the final weeks of the
war but were so famished they no longer had the energy to fight.

Thousands of Biafran soldiers took off their uniforms and joined the hordes roaming the bush in search of food.

An end to the drama came not through the efforts of international aid workers but with Ojukwu's escape to Ivory Coast in January 1970. Nigerian government troops at his heels, he fled with his wife, children, 3,000 kilos of luggage and his white Mercedes-Benz in a plane that took off from Uli. Biafra had ceased to exist, but Ojukwu lived happily ever after, first in Ivory Coast, later back in Nigeria, thanks in part to his bank accounts in Zurich and London.

To this day the humanitarian world has its doubts. Did the humanitarians prolong the Biafran war by a year and a half by giving moral and financial support to Ojukwu? And do they therefore share the responsibility for the death by starvation of hundreds of thousands of people? Or did they help to prevent genocide?

Throughout the war, the mother of all aid organizations, the International Committee of the Red Cross, stuck firmly to its conviction that humanitarian responsibility must extend beyond the drama of the moment. It pointed to the principles of neutrality enshrined in the Geneva Conventions, which stipulate that humanitarian aid workers must operate independently of warring parties, and behind the scenes it engaged in negotiations on options and conditions that would ensure the aid benefited the victims and not Ojukwu's soldiers. A number of ICRC doctors watched in frustration as other aid organizations disregarded the principle of neutrality, openly condemned the 'genocide' and mobilized to help Biafra. By keeping silent, 'we doctors were accomplices in the systematic massacre of a population', wrote French doctor Bernard Kouchner, who led the group of disillusioned humanitarians.[3] They broke away from the ICRC and founded Médecins sans Frontières in 1971.

After Ojukwu fled, President Gowon of Nigeria banned a number of aid organizations from returning to Biafra. He growled: 'Let them keep their blood money, let them keep their bloody relief supplies.'

★

Famine is rarely caused by a lack of food. It far more frequently occurs because people are denied the right to food. As Nobel Prize-winning economist Amartya Sen points out, 'Functioning democratic societies do not tend to have famines.'[4]

After Biafra, ethical questions about supplying aid in the case of a deliberately generated and sustained famine were left unanswered, while the need for an answer became ever more urgent. In fifteen of the twenty-seven countries that required emergency food aid in 2007 – in other words more than half – the cause lay in civil war. The WFP gives Darfur, southern Sudan, Angola, northern Uganda, Congo and West Africa as prominent recent examples (dating from 1995 or since).[5]

Warring parties know the advantages of the hunger weapon and deploy it whenever and wherever they can. Yet the provision of three-quarters of all food aid worldwide is left to private aid organizations that have no shared, binding ethical agreements and that are not asked, let alone required, to have any understanding of exactly what the conflicts in which they distribute the 'food weapon' are about.

Again and again the same problem raises its ugly head. In former Yugoslavia, ethnic cleansing was the central war aim and food aid a strategic instrument. If those in power locally gave aid organizations permission to distribute food aid in a particular region, it was because populations had to be persuaded to stay put. In areas where permission was denied, the purpose of the ban was to force people to leave.

'At the main Serb checkpoint outside Sarajevo, the big Human to Human aid convoy stood stalled in its tracks. Sweating profusely, a uniformed Serb fighter pushed a wheelbarrow full of goods taken from one of the vehicles into the cellar of the house he and his comrades were using as a guardroom. Nearby, other Serb fighters were stacking cartons of the seized aid into a minivan,' writes journalist Marita Vihervuori of the Austrian Press Agency in the book *Crimes of War 2.0*. Nevertheless, the Human to Human convoy was one of the few private aid convoys that ever made it to Sarajevo.

It was stripped of still more of its load in the Serb-controlled suburb of Ilidza. 'In the end, only the flour and the macaroni made it into the city.'[6]

On some routes 80 per cent of the aid was seized. The UNHCR stubbornly continued to send convoys, 'in the interests of the victims'. 'We couldn't let the people there die, so we closed our eyes to a lot of things,' a UNHCR representative in Zagreb explained later.

Slobodan Milosevic used food aid in his attack on ethnic Albanians in Kosovo. He starved the Albanians by systematically making it impossible for them to acquire food by their own efforts (his troops burned food stocks and prevented farmers from sowing and harvesting) and then ordered his men to loot the warehouses used by humanitarian organizations that came to help the Kosovars.

A Danish aid convoy on its way to a Muslim enclave in Bosnia got stuck at a roadblock manned by Croat fighters. It was 1994. The Croats were strategically starving Muslims in the enclaves. 'We are not taking sides: our aid is neutral,' a Danish aid worker said in an attempt to negotiate a way through for the convoy. One of the Croat fighters merely burst out laughing. 'You say you are helping women and children. You are doing nothing of the sort. You are helping the Muslims,' he snarled at the Dane.[7]

In the War on Terror, Western military commanders use the hunger weapon if it suits them. In the spring of 2004, for instance, American coalition troops closed the roads to the Iraqi city of Fallujah and put its residents 'on rations' to force the insurgents among them to surrender. The Iraqi Red Crescent organization tried to deliver drinking water, but the US army kept the city sealed off until the enemy succumbed. In September that year, during the attack on Tall Afar, coalition soldiers used the same tactic, and they did so again a month later in Samarra.

Humanitarian principles are diametrically opposed to the basic principle of war, which is simple: warring parties want to win, 'our own' included. At any price. In May 1996 the then US ambassador to the United Nations, Madeleine Albright, was a guest on the CBS television programme *Sixty Minutes*. The discussion focused on the American embargo against Iraq, designed to bring Saddam Hussein to his knees. *Sixty Minutes* presenter Lesley Stahl put it to Albright that half a million children had already died because of the shortages of food and medicines brought about by the embargo. 'That's more children than died in Hiroshima. And – you know, is the price worth it?' she asked.

'I think this is a very hard choice,' Albright replied. 'But the price – we think the price is worth it.'

Even humanitarian aid organizations deploy the hunger weapon if it serves their purposes. In East Timor at the time of the UN transitional administration in 1999, Dutch journalist Tjitske Lingsma met a UNICEF worker who, 'while bent over a plate of fried noodles, said it was a good idea not to distribute too much food in the capital, Dili. He wanted to keep the capital slightly hungry, as a way of preventing too many people from moving to Dili.'

In 1992 the WFP offered leaders in north-eastern Somalia deliveries of food aid. In that part of Somalia there was unrest but no famine. Local leaders found themselves confronting a major dilemma. Because the people did not need the food to survive on, they would sell it and buy weapons with the proceeds. Yet refusing food aid wasn't an option, since hostile clans, who were not starving either, had accepted the offer and were using the income from selling the supplies to arm themselves. The result was an arms race, and soon no community had any choice but to take part.

---

8. When recipients call the shots

The rebels are like fish, the villages are like water to fish.
We pump their ponds away.

Ahmad Harun, Sudanese Minister of State for Humanitarian Affairs,
in 2004, on ethnic cleansing in Darfur

Harun announced to anyone who cared to listen that he had 'the power and authority to kill or forgive whoever in Darfur'. In 2007 an arrest warrant was issued for him by the International Criminal Court (ICC) in The Hague. He is said to have incited the Janjaweed militias on more than one occasion to carry out attacks on civilians.

The end of the Cold War brought freedom, not least for international aid organizations. The division of the world into East and West had made wars more or less private encounters between the superpowers, with aid organizations working mainly on the periphery, in refugee camps at the edges of war zones, for instance. Since 1989 and the fall of the Berlin Wall, the warring parties themselves have stood at the gates to their 'humanitarian territories'. When it comes to the best ways of making sure INGOs are of service to them in the new world order, and of milking them dry, many a brazen ethnic or religious nationalist could learn a lesson or two from the leaders of Ethiopia and Sudan.

Persistent drought was only one of the causes of the 1984 great famine in Ethiopia. More significant were the civil wars between government soldiers and rebels in the northern provinces of Eritrea and Tigray. The rebels were holding out with the help of their supporters in the villages, who supplied them with food, water, hiding places and fresh recruits. The Stalinesque regime of Mengistu Haile Mariam spotted an opportunity to kill two birds with one stone. By driving villagers out of the north and towards the south, into government-held territory, he could rob the rebels of their support, while the vast state-owned agricultural enterprises in the south of the country would receive a huge influx of cheap, if not free, labour.

Government soldiers sealed off the northern region and went to work. They shot men and boys dead. They raped and mutilated women and girls. They flung infants on to fires alive. They set schools and clinics ablaze, slaughtered livestock, burned grain stores and poisoned water sources with human corpses and dead animals.

Once the famine was a fact and floods of refugees were on the move, the regime invited the international media to come and film the 'humanitarian drama'. Millions were close to death. 'Because of drought,' government spokesmen said in interviews. The solution, according to the regime, was to set up reception camps for the survivors and evacuate them from there to the south, away from the drought-stricken region. For such a massive operation the regime needed money. The images of starving northern Ethiopian children sent back by BBC correspondent Michael Buerk and cameraman Mohammed Amin in October 1984 were the starting signal for an international fundraising campaign.

The BBC had agreed to show 'famine footage' on behalf of the Disasters Emergency Committee (DEC), an umbrella organization that brings together aid agencies including the British Red Cross, Save the Children and Oxfam. Like some other journalists in Ethiopia at the time, Buerk considered the war in Ethiopia a 'side story' that would complicate relief efforts. A story about victims of drought would raise more money than one about 'yet another stupid African war', as Buerk put it years later. On 23 October 2004 journalist Daniel Wolf wrote in the *Spectator*:

When I spoke to Michael Buerk in the late 1990s, he [. . .] held the view that wars had 'complicated matters'. [. . .] He did agree that self-censorship had played a role in his own and others' reportage at the time: 'You've got [. . .] to make the decision, is this side story of any real significance?

And also, at the back of your mind, is: if I overemphasise a negative angle to this, I am going to be responsible for [. . .] inhibiting people from coughing up their money.'

The two most important donor governments in those years, Great Britain, led by Margaret Thatcher, and the US, with Ronald Reagan at the helm, refused to assist the 'revolutionary' regime in Ethiopia in any way. They sent neither funding nor food aid. Private aid organizations spontaneously joined forces with pop stars to plug the financial gap. In December 1984, some two months after Buerk's television reports, the song 'Do They Know It's Christmas?' by Bob Geldof's Operation Band Aid entered the charts at number one all over the Western world. The proceeds from record sales, around £8 million, were intended for 'the victims of drought' in Ethiopia. In July 1985 Geldof's Live Aid concerts followed, at venues across Europe and in the US. 'Feeding Africa' became a great apolitical crusade. The total amount the Aid artists sung out of their audience was more than £90 million. The money, coming from private donors, was spent by private INGOs – this time not in compliance with conditions laid down by donor governments but instead those of the recipient, the Ethiopian regime. Thousands of Western aid workers and journalists flew in along with the money. They were forced to change their dollars for local currency at rates favourable to the regime, and this alone helped to keep the Ethiopian war machine running. Food aid from INGOs was used as bait to lure starving villagers into camps. They were held there awaiting deportation to the state farms in the south. A life of forced labour lay ahead. The government army that guarded the camps took a share of the food aid and even requisitioned trucks from aid organizations to move people out.

The compulsory trip southwards took an average of five days. About 600,000 people were moved and an estimated 100,000 of them perished on the way. In November 1985 the *Irish Times* put that figure to the initiator of Live Aid, Bob Geldof. The singer shrugged. 'In the context [of the famine], these numbers don't shock me,' he told the reporter. The fact that aid was available was more important than the circumstances in which it had to be delivered. 'If Live Aid had existed during the Second World War, and if we'd heard that there were people dying in concentration camps, would we have refused to bring food and assistance to those camps? Of course not!' he said.[1] But as would undoubtedly have been the case in Nazi Germany, in Ethiopia the management of the camps decided how much of the aid went to its own staff and how much to the prisoners.

In some camps where deportations met with resistance, government troops shut the INGOs' food distribution centres, so that people became hungry again and changed their minds. In other camps INGOs were forbidden to feed the starving children of parents who put up a struggle. When around 6,000 children died of starvation in one camp in late 1985 even though there was enough food for them, MSF France could bear it no longer. Comparing Ethiopia to Cambodia under the Khmer Rouge, the organization left the country.

Other aid agencies averted their eyes, withstood growing criticism in Western newspapers and remained in Ethiopia, taking exception to 'cynical attempts' by their critics to 'politicize aid'.

The Dutch Ecumenical Aid Foundation (SOH) and the Dutch Red Cross were among them. To the reproach that aid organizations were allowing themselves to be manipulated by the regime, an SOH spokesman said, 'I regard that as an extremely unfair accusation. And I think it does an injustice to the primary aim of humanitarian organizations: to help people in need.' In the indignation expressed by the head of international affairs for the Dutch Red Cross a similar echo of Henri Dunant could be heard: 'Politics evades its responsibility and then humanitarian aid organizations are reproached for keeping the war going?!'[2]

In its analysis of events, Oxfam, one of the largest of the INGOs on the ground, went no further than to raise questions about the 'haste, scale and timing' of the government's migration programme. 'Do They Know It's Christmas?' and the Live Aid concerts had doubled Oxfam's turnover inside a year to more than £50 million. No one knows for certain how many lives were ultimately lost during the 'rescue operation' for the people of northern Ethiopia. Estimates vary from as many as 1 million to as 'few' as 300,000.

Around the same time as the cleansing operation in northern Ethiopia, the neighbouring Sudanese regime implemented a similar strategy in southern Sudan. There too were rebels whose supporters had to be driven out of their villages. In 1982 the army and militias invaded the area, kicking off a terror campaign that would last for years. Villages went up in flames. Millions fled for their lives, initially further southwards, then over the border into northern Kenya and Ethiopia. Many refugees ended up in dirty, overpopulated enclaves on Sudanese soil, sealed off by government troops. 'Peace Villages' they were called. Their inhabitants were said to be victims of 'drought'.

In 1989 the regime, the rebels and the United Nations signed an agreement to deliver supplies to the Peace Villages. This was allowed only from the air. And the sacks of food were to be pushed out of planes only over areas approved by the regime.

To implement Operation Lifeline Sudan, as it was called, the UN and at least thirty-five INGOs descended on the hot, dusty deserts of northern Kenya. The remote settlement of Lokichoggio was transformed into a thrumming logistical hub. With $1 million a day to spend, the humanitarian operation was the largest and most expensive in the world at the time. It was to become one of the lengthiest in the history of humanitarianism. Hercules transport planes took off from the landing strip in Lokichoggio with thousands of kilos of food aid on board, year in year out, until well into the new millennium, several times a day, seven days a week.

Controlled as it was by the Sudanese regime, the operation resembled nothing so much as the management of a hydroponics greenhouse, where the grower determines which plants get water and how much by opening or closing the drip system. 'Weekly updates' sent back to donors by the humanitarians in Lokichoggio gave a detailed account of all the latest restrictions imposed on them by the regime: '9 July 1997 – Permission received for aid flights to population centres with the exception of Yei, Tali, Maridi, Yirol, Rumbek, Tonj, Warrap and Kongor.' The Sudanese government had decided it was unnecessary for people in those particular Peace Villages to receive any food that week. When the regime imposed a ban of several months on dropping aid anywhere in the southern region of Bahr el Ghazal, an estimated 60,000 people starved to death.

The aid organizations had little if any means of finding out exactly what was happening to the food they did have permission to drop. Sometimes messages reached Lokichoggio about the bombing of food distribution points; food aid had apparently served as bait to entice enemies of the regime. From time to time Peace Villages were attacked shortly after receiving supplies and the sacks of rice were carried off by pro-government militias.

One thing was certain. The government army was feeding itself on food aid. Alex de Waal, former researcher for Human Rights Watch, concluded that the army had managed to hold its ground in a number of strategically important towns, Juba especially, thanks in part to the provision of aid by humanitarian organizations. Food drops by Lifeline saved Juba from falling to the rebels on several occasions. Rebels had surrounded the town and were preventing supplies of food from reaching government forces by road.

The rebels too made off with all the aid they could lay their hands on, which was one reason they were able to go on fighting.

A reporter for the *New York Times* asked an American diplomat serving in Sudan whether aid was keeping the war in southern Sudan going. 'Absolutely, absolutely,' he answered.[3]

Yet what was needed to relieve human suffering in southern Sudan, the humanitarians believed, was more aid. In Britain the Disasters Emergency Committee launched a fundraising drive. 'Lack of timely rain and displacement of people prevents farmers from cultivation,' was how the UN explained the suffering to potential donors. Millions of pounds were paid into the DEC account.

The food aid that rained down upon the Sudanese civil war was worth hundreds of millions of dollars, but whoever Operation Lifeline saved, they weren't necessarily civilians. 'In any war, the last ones to die of hunger will be the soldiers,' a spokesman for the World Food Programme said. 'It's frustrating, damn frustrating.' A report written by Dr Millard Burr for the US Committee for Refugees in 1998, after nearly ten years of Lifeline, concluded:

1.9 million of the 2 million deaths since 1983 were a direct result of intentional policies of the Sudan government. They were attributable to war-related famine and disease, and Sudanese government policies that spread conflict, forced southern Sudanese to relocate, and blocked relief efforts by the United Nations and international relief agencies.[4]

The money the regime was able to save on provisioning its soldiers and militiamen was spent, among other things, on its next military adventure. Rebels in the Nubian mountains had to be robbed of their support. People were driven out of their villages by murder, rape, torture, the burning of fields, felling of fruit trees and poisoning of water sources. At least 100,000 people died, perhaps 200,000, and another 100,000 fled to new filthy Peace Villages. There too INGOs were permitted to supply food. But again only when, where and to the extent that the regime allowed.

At around the same time, in the spring of 1999, a fresh invitation from the regime in Ethiopia landed on the desks of international journalists. Would they like to come and take a look at the latest famine? Again in the Ogaden. Again 'caused by drought'. In reality: another cleansing operation. There was still enough water in the Ogaden, but most wells either belonged to private landowners, who were charging high fees for their use, or were controlled by the army, in which case only supporters of the regime could drink from them.

In the umpteenth instalment of the same long-running horror serial, the area was sealed off, men and boys murdered, women and girls raped, and infants flung on to fires alive. Schools, clinics and grain stores went up in flames and livestock were slaughtered.

International camera teams were flown to the town of Gode in the Ogaden from the Ethiopian capital, Addis Ababa. Virtually every report on the famine of 1999 came from within a fifty-kilometre radius of Gode. The journalists all took up the same offer of a day trip to the cemetery in the village of Denang. The journey took them along a road next to which dead cows lay decomposing. The cadavers had been dragged there and laid in plain view specially for the press.

Standing beside the fresh graves of children, local government officials made speeches. The starvation was the fault of the international community, they said, which knew it hadn't rained in three years and yet had not acted.

The WFP turned to donor governments with a request for food aid for 1 million victims. The regime 'corrected' that figure to 2 million. That same week Ethiopia's leaders adjusted the number of people affected to 4 million and a little later via 8 million to 16 million. The Ogaden is home to no more than 4 million people, but the aid world said nothing. The WFP simply revised its original request and asked for donations that would allow it to feed 'the whole of northern Ethiopia'. Because of 'drought'.

Donors shipped in 900,000 tons of grain altogether. Its distribution, organized under military supervision, enabled the government to gain firm control of areas where the army's grip had previously been weak. The Ogaden became one huge sealed-off military camp. Distribution was supervised by government troops. The INGOs in the area were kept on a tight leash: bureaucratic approval procedures for work permits took months; organizations were allowed to bring only a limited number of vehicles to the Ogaden; the use of heavy lorries, helicopters and satellite phones was forbidden and steep import taxes were levied on aid supplies. In their internal reports, INGOs themselves estimated that 20–30 per cent of the total value of the aid, which they put at $70 million, was seized by soldiers. Among other signs, they had noticed soldiers at local markets selling grain, oil and biscuits taken from aid rations.

In 2003 it was again the turn of the Sudanese regime, which this time invited the international humanitarian community to come to western Sudan. All the elements of the familiar story were there: soldiers, militias and rebels; murder, arson, looting, rape and mutilation. Two hundred thousand people died; 2 million survivors were driven into grimy, overcrowded camps. INGOs were permitted to supply aid to them on terms laid down by the regime. Thirteen UN organizations and more than 130 INGOs large and small responded to the invitation. The name of the latest 'humanitarian territory' was Darfur.

Today, anyone who looks past the camps and focuses instead on the Sudanese capital of Khartoum will see that things are going well for the regime. Majestic new bridges are being built across the Nile and office blocks are going up. Young, rich Sudanese in fashionable training shoes with designer rips in their jeans hurry along the city's boulevards to the countless supermarkets and hypermarkets in the centre of town, where they are confronted with a choice between fourteen different scents of toilet freshener and an assortment of imported frozen delicacies. Since 2003 sales figures for plasma televisions and for BMWs priced at $160,000 have rocketed in Khartoum. The latest gadgets to hit the capital are outdoor air-conditioning systems, much in demand among the owners of the city's cafés and restaurants. While the rest of Khartoum swelters at over 40° Celsius, these ingenious air-cooling machines wrap drinkers and diners on outdoor terraces in cool, romantic drifts of mist.

Sudan's economy is booming. The regime extracts more than 500,000 barrels of oil a day – a mere drip compared to the production of countries such as Saudi Arabia, but enough to generate a daily income for the state of roughly $1 million. What the regime saves on servicing camps for displaced persons it can spend on Chinese

FN-6 rocket launchers, Russian attack helicopters and other military paraphernalia. At the time of the mass killings in Darfur, more than 70 per cent of the national income went on defence.

In 2005 the Sudanese government signed a peace agreement with the rebels in the south. The ceremony was followed by a donor conference in Oslo at which the regime was allocated over $4 billion for reconstruction in the war-ravaged region. That was more than half the total amount being spent annually on emergency humanitarian aid throughout the world at the time. The donor plan provided for the arrival of around fifty INGOs, but the regime determined the conditions under which they were allowed to work.

'Some food-aid flights are refused permission to take off and others are not permitted to land, and our cars and trucks are detained at the border,' the UN reported soon after the operation began. Sudan was the largest recipient of humanitarian assistance in 2008 and received $1.3 billion from the OECD member states alone.

A fair wind is blowing for the Ethiopian regime too.

Sat between a beaming Tony Blair and Sir Bob Geldof, Ethiopia's Prime Minister, Meles Zenawi, could hardly have wished for a stronger endorsement. The launch of Mr Blair's Commission for Africa report in March 2005 in Ethiopia's capital, Addis Ababa, enhanced Mr Meles's position as the British Government's – and the West's – favourite African leader. Handpicked by Mr Blair to sit on the commission, Mr Meles was viewed as the man to lead the 'African renaissance'. He was seen as a leader committed to development and democracy. Britain still gives Ethiopia £130m in humanitarian aid each year – more than any other African country. Like the US, Britain has tried to retain a relatively close relationship with Ethiopia – one of its few allies in a volatile Horn of Africa.[5]

After Sudan and Afghanistan, Ethopia was the third largest recipient of official humanitarian assistance in 2008. It received $807 million. The regime has also worked the country up to the status of second largest recipient of food aid in the world after North Korea. Around

300 NGOs have permanent offices in Addis Ababa; at least a hundred of them would not exist but for their contracts to distribute food aid.

The EU and the US send more than 1 million tons of grain every year. The logistics are a goldmine for Ethiopian ministers: they own the trucks that drive to Ethiopia and back, day in, day out, from the port of Mombasa in Kenya.

The question 'Do They Know It's Christmas?' is more irrelevant than ever, but from time to time its echoes can still be heard. In November 2004 the BBC's Michael Buerk was one of the speakers in a panel discussion held by the Royal African Society in London. He described his most recent visit to Ethiopia, twenty years after he shot his 'famine footage' in the north of the country. In a report of the meeting on the African Society website we read:

Buerk began with the disclaimer that he was not a reporter nor a food expert or politician, that he was barely clever enough to ask the questions but far too stupid to answer them. He was neither a supporter nor a detractor of the Ethiopian government but had the opinion that it was one of the more 'interesting' governments in Africa and Meles Zenawi [who helped overthrow Mengistu Haile Mariam in 1991] one of the cleverest leaders he had met.

In March 2005 a Dutch aid worker in southern Ethiopia, employed by a German development aid organization, came upon several northern Ethiopians who had been put on transports back in 1984. Loaded on to trucks by government soldiers toting machine-guns, the unfortunates had been driven to his agricultural project to work as forced labourers.

In 2007 the Ogaden was sealed off again. Men were murdered, women and girls raped and infants strangled or tossed alive on to fires. Schools and clinics were shelled or set alight, livestock slaughtered and grain stores burned. Two hundred thousand people fled; some were forced into Peace Villages.

★

In July 2008 the International Criminal Court asked the UN Security Council to issue an arrest warrant for the Sudanese president, Omar Hassan al-Bashir. The judges charged Bashir with war crimes and crimes against humanity for playing an 'essential role' in the murder, rape, torture, pillaging and displacement of a large number of civilians in Darfur.

Some experts say that as many as 450,000 people died in Darfur, and that the government campaign essentially rearranged the demographics of this vast region, displacing nearly half the population.

The INGOs in Sudan are the milch-cows of Bashir's state apparatus. In 2008 an employee of an American INGO explained to me how it works. She wanted to remain anonymous to avoid causing problems for her colleagues.

It's an open secret among donors, UN organizations and INGOs that the government earns several million dollars a quarter on visas, travel permits, work permits for humanitarians and permit extensions. Entering Sudan costs. Leaving Sudan: ditto. Foreigners aren't allowed to be based anywhere but in Khartoum. To visit or work in any location outside of Khartoum you need a permit. A cost. I worked for twenty months in Kassala in the north-east. My INGO had to reapply for a permit for me every two months, and pay for it. All permits are issued for short periods of time, sometimes for two months, sometimes as long as six months but sometimes for only a month, whatever the official decides. Extensions are often delayed or refused in order to intimidate INGO staff.

To set up an INGO you need approval from HAC, which is part of the Humanitarian Affairs Ministry. The minister is Ahmad Harun, indicted by the ICC for crimes against humanity. Registering an INGO costs money and at every stage of the application process you pay again. Every INGO oils the wheels of the regime with cash and gifts. One gift that's much in demand is that you give someone a job.

Once an INGO is registered, there's the problem of procuring equipment and personnel. INGOs are not allowed to advertise for staff. That has to be done through HAC, who also do the applicant short-listing, sit on the interview panel and decide who gets hired. The net effect is that all international organizations employ regime informants, and that includes the UN and the diplomatic missions in Sudan.

All INGOs have to deduct income tax and pay national insurance contributions. All that money goes to the Ministry of Finance.

The Communications Ministry profits as well. INGOs aren't allowed to use their own satellite communications systems (VSATs). Instead they have to apply to the ministry for a communications permit, and pay for it. Once they have one they can sign up with an ISP for internet and rent phone lines. All the telecoms companies and the providers are either directly government owned or owned by members of the regime. Anyone who wants to have a Thuraya [satellite phone] has to ask for a permit too. The fees run to thousands of dollars, since the regime wants to deter people from using Thurayas. The permits have to be renewed annually.

Then there are the import duties. Most of the things INGOs need for humanitarian purposes have to come from abroad. Car and truck batteries, generators, every little bit of Western technology – the import duties double the price of every product. All the aid supplies the INGOs import are taxed too, which also helps to fill the regime's coffers. In theory, aid supplies are exempt from VAT, but not in practice. The World Food Programme fought a constant lonely battle about not paying import duty on its food consignments arriving at Port Sudan and destined for Darfur. All the other INGOs pay without complaint, even for things like medicines and insecticide-treated mosquito nets. My own INGO waited for two years for permission to import the vehicles we needed duty-free. Without that exemption we'd have had to pay double the price for every vehicle. The alternative was to rent. At extortionate prices. In Khartoum there are hundreds of car-hire companies in the hands of associates of the regime.

I could go on, but you get the picture. Add up the thousands of aid workers in the country and with all those permits and duties you get a significant income for the state.

It drives me wild that the 'humanitarian community' is so spineless in its dealings with the regime. If there was some collective spirit, we might be able to avoid becoming in effect sub-branches of the Sudan state. But all INGO leaders play the game. They don't want to risk their work permits. After all, they're not paying out of their own pockets and they're only in the country temporarily, so all this will outlast their time here.

Only thirty minutes after the ICC ordered the arrest of President Bashir, the regime retaliated with an order for thirteen INGOs to leave Darfur and the north of the country immediately. Forty per cent of the 17,000 aid workers present in these parts of the country – 7,610 persons, of whom 308 were foreigners – packed their bags. Oxfam GB and the Dutch and French chapters of MSF were among the banned organizations.

Dutch journalist and Sudan expert Arita Baaijens interviewed some of them in London and Amsterdam in 2009 and 2010.

When the regime ordered the thirteen INGOs out, it froze their bank accounts. The INGOs were forced to leave their Land Cruisers, laptops, computers, printers, modems, satellite phones and office furniture behind, too. Oxfam GB lost €5.5 million, €2.3 million of it in possessions and accounts. MSF France admitted to having lost €2 million. All thirteen INGOs were fined and served with after-taxes.

None of the INGOs nor the donor governments protested. Not openly anyhow. Soon it became clear why they kept silent: they all hoped to be allowed to return to Sudan. American INGOs were. Following a quick meeting between members of the regime and the American envoy for the Sudan, Scott Gration, Save the Children USA and three other American organizations were allowed back, but under different names.

'Why would INGOs want to come back?' asked Arita Baaijens after visiting Darfur in November 2009. 'They can't go anywhere. For every step they want to take outside their offices they need a permit. In practice, they're under "office arrest".'

People in Darfur shared their suspicions with Baaijens that money is the reason. With around a billion donor dollars per year, including private donations, the aid operation in Darfur is the largest in the world.

The banned INGOs admitted to Arita Baaijens that in their talks with the Sudanese regime, they were negotiating the rules and conditions under which they would perhaps be allowed back. They were just hoping for the best. They were not discussing among themselves a joint strategy against the regime's conditions. The humanitarians Baaijens interviewed in Darfur, London and Amsterdam agreed with her that their organizations had learned nothing from this episode.

'Of course we're creating a precedent by allowing this to happen,' said Vanessa van Schoor of MSF Holland. 'But to stay away from Darfur was not an option,' she added. 'People there need us.'

9. Afghaniscam

The more they help us find the bad guys, the more good stuff they get.

Lieutenant Reid 'Huck' Finn of the US army, as he hands out
blankets, shirts and sewing kits to displaced Afghans in Dwamanda,
close to the border with Pakistan[1]

Ground Zero in Manhattan, New York, is still a gaping hole seven
years after the attacks of 11 September 2001. Happily spooked
tourists stare through the wire-mesh fence. Street vendors encircle
them, pointedly waving photos of the burning towers. A full album
changes hands for $7. For roughly the same amount you can buy a
snowglobe with the Twin Towers in it, or a T-shirt with the towers
on. A few quarters will get you a hot-dog from the cart next to the
fence.

I content myself with a nice Ground Zero baseball cap.

'We are a country awakened to danger and called to defend freedom,'
George W. Bush blazed immediately after the attack in a speech
broadcast worldwide.

We will direct every resource at our command – every means of diplomacy,
every tool of intelligence, every instrument of law enforcement, every
financial influence, and every necessary weapon of war – to the disruption
and to the defeat of the global terror network. Our grief has turned to
anger, and anger to resolution. Justice will be done![2]

Colin Powell, then Bush's Secretary of State, wasted no time in
detailing what the American government expected from American
aid organizations under this new policy – if they were hoping to
have their federal funding extended, that is. 'Just as surely as our
diplomats and military, American NGOs are out there serving and

sacrificing on the front lines of freedom. NGOs are such a force multiplier for us, such an important part of our combat team,' he said in a speech.[3]

USAID, which manages the American government's aid budget, repeated the message yet again. On 21 May 2003, in Washington, Andrew Natsios, the former head of USAID, gave a speech. Naomi Klein wrote in the *Guardian* that he was

blasting US NGOs for failing to play a role many of them didn't realize they had been assigned: doing public relations for the US government.

According to InterAction, the network of 160 relief and development NGOs, Natsios was 'irritated' that starving and sick Iraqi and Afghan children didn't realize that their food and vaccines were coming to them courtesy of George Bush. From now on, NGOs had to do a better job of linking their humanitarian assistance to US foreign policy and making it clear that they are 'an arm of the US government'. If they didn't [...] 'Natsios threatened to personally tear up their contracts and find new partners.[4]

The American administration expected other governments to steer the same course. 'Either you are with us, or you are with the terrorists,' Bush said in his speech. In 2004, after handing in his resignation, Richard Armitage, the number two in Bush's State Department under Colin Powell, summed up America's post-9/11 foreign policy as 'Listen, fucker, you do what we say.'

European countries did indeed rush to rally around America. After 9/11 the European Commission put its aid budgets 'at the service of Europe's security policy'. Member states of the Organ--isation for Economic Co-operation and Development (OECD) sided with the Americans too. They, the thirty richest donor governments, made it known that from then on their aid budgets had 'an important role to play' in depriving terrorists of grass-roots support.[5] They referred to the 'breeding ground theory': from poverty comes discontent and from discontent comes terrorism.

Since 9/11, Iraq and Afghanistan have been among the biggest recipients of Official Development Assistance from the OECD, and of relief funds donated by Europe and the US. Iraq became the largest and most expensive American aid project since the Marshall Plan for Europe that followed the Second World War; Afghanistan, the second largest.

In October 2001, a month after 9/11, American warplanes bombed the Taliban in Afghanistan. The War on Terror had begun. The Taliban was driven back, partly into neighbouring Pakistan, but not defeated. When the air strikes were over, a cavalcade of military and civilian aid workers from more than sixty countries moved into Afghanistan to help reconstruct the country.

Visiting Afghanistan in 2007, I encounter a humanitarian community in deep crisis. The humanitarians turn out to be living in fear, of the Taliban, which is stalking the entire country once more, and of roadside bombs and kidnappings.

After they land at Kabul, donor delegations calling in on Afghanistan to see how their aid projects are progressing are immediately driven at high speed in bullet-proof vehicles to NATO headquarters in the city, where they take cover behind sandbags and razor wire. Their visits rarely last more than a day – often just a few hours. After talking with a few NGO coordinators drummed up for the occasion they may stay just long enough to have lunch with Afghan members of parliament, for example, but then they rush back to the airport. Planes taking off from Kabul climb steeply to get beyond the range of any Taliban rocket launchers as quickly as possible.

At the NATO base too, people are frightened. Most NATO soldiers in Kabul aren't even allowed to leave the camp. In his whole tour of duty, three months so far, one of the soldiers I speak to has spent a total of just six hours outside the gates, on hasty trips to the airport to pick up parcels and envelopes for his commanding officer. 'Walls and the screen of my laptop are all I ever see,' the Dutch corporal tells me sadly. He resorts to reading books about the country to gain something of a feel for the Afghan atmosphere. He's just finished *The Kite Runner* by Khaled Hosseini.

Diplomats posted to Kabul don't dare go out either. A member of staff at the Dutch embassy confides in me that the team lives and works within the guarded walls of the embassy. If people venture beyond the gates at all, they have a strong preference for doing so in armoured vehicles.

And you can search till you're blue in the face for the more than 300 INGOs in Kabul. They hide. In every other crisis zone they make a show of their presence, with colours and slogans proudly displayed on T-shirts, caps, office frontages and car aerials, but in the War on Terror they almost all get by without even the tiniest logos on the doors to their houses and cars. They manage their aid projects from behind thick, anonymous, metres-high walls topped with razor wire, surrounded by sandbags and concrete-filled oil drums.

The job of humanitarian aid worker is number five on the top-ten list of dangerous occupations, after lumberjack, pilot, fisherman, and structural iron and steel worker. It's the only job on the list where most of the fatalities are caused by intentional violence. According to aid organizations, this is because the situation has confused the locals. Since the start of the War on Terror and the military–humanitarian reconstruction projects in front-line states, they say, people can no longer tell the difference between 'real', neutral humanitarians and reconstruction troops disguised as humanitarians. Violence against aid workers – not just in countries such as Afghanistan and Iraq but in Somalia, Sudan and Chad, for example – is really aimed, the aid agencies say, at soldiers of the US army, NATO, the African Union, EUFOR (European Union Forces), the United Nations and anyone else engaged in 'peacekeeping', 'humanitarian intervention' or 'winning hearts and minds' in those front-line states.

But in 2004 the British Overseas Development Institute (ODI) investigated the background to serious violence against aid workers in operations like these and concluded, among other things, that 'careful study of such cases suggests one aim of the perpetrators was to [. . .] punish aid workers for political or strategic reasons'. INGOs funded by the American government are expected to act as 'force multipliers'. INGOs in receipt of European money are meant to serve European security policy. And with funding from the OECD, INGOs are supposed to run projects, or facilitate the running of projects, that are aimed in part at depriving terrorists of their grass-roots support. If such military and political intentions lie behind the giving of aid, then surely it's far from unreasonable if aid is received with equally military and political intentions in mind. Warring parties at the receiving end are not dumb, deaf or blind. Like those who give it, they see aid as an instrument of war and therefore regard aid workers collectively as part of the opposing force.

In 2004 the death of five staff members of MSF Holland in Afghanistan was a clear and horrifying demonstration of this confusion between humanitarianism and military intervention. In his subsequent research into the role of aid agencies in Afghanistan, Fabrice Weissman, research director for the MSF Foundation in Paris, was harshly critical of the elision that had taken place in the country. It is worth quoting at length from his report:

When all is said and done, the only protection humanitarian actors have is the clarity of their image. Both coalition forces and the majority of aid actors have seriously abused this image in Afghanistan, thus perpetuating a deadly confusion between humanitarian organizations and political–military institutions.

In Afghanistan, the first aspect of this confusion was caused by camouflaging psychological warfare and intelligence operations as humanitarian action. Clear-cut examples include the coalition's 'humanitarian' food drops during the first aerial strikes in 2001, its deployment of special forces in civilian dress who claim to be on a 'humanitarian mission', and threatening to suspend humanitarian aid to populations in southern Afghanistan if they refuse to provide information about the Taliban and Al-Qaeda.

Winning the hearts and minds of civilian populations and encouraging them to cooperate with military forces are classic and legal military techniques according to the Geneva Conventions. On the other hand, presenting a combat tactic as a humanitarian operation blatantly violates the humanitarian symbol, just as using a Red Cross vehicle to transport weapons clandestinely alongside a patient would be.

After the defeat of the Taliban, many institutional donors required NGOs and UN agencies to help stabilize and rebuild Afghanistan. The vast majority of humanitarian actors placed themselves at the service of the UN Assistance Mission in Afghanistan (UNAMA) and of the interim government. Both of these actors receive varying degrees of support from coalition forces.

NGOs and UN agencies thus abandoned the independence essential to providing independent aid and modeled their priorities on those of the new regime and its Western allies, who were still at war with the Taliban.

This scenario constitutes the second element of confusion: making it impossible to distinguish between a subcontractor working on behalf of a warring party and an independent, impartial humanitarian aid actor.

Finally, the use of humanitarian rhetoric to justify going to war is another confusing element. Beyond retaliation for the 11 September attacks, the defense of human rights and international humanitarian law were presented as forceful arguments in favor of armed intervention in Afghanistan. The world was told that force and occupation were required to save an exhausted population from famine, to improve women's access to medical care and to ease refugees' return, among other goals.

This martial and imperial use of humanitarian rhetoric contributed significantly to blurring the image of aid organizations. If an appeal to humanitarian considerations can justify both a medical aid operation and a military campaign, doesn't that suggest that aid workers and international troops represent two sides of the same coin?[6]

Nevertheless INGOs cling, apparently unperturbed, to their claim to a neutral, 'non-governmental' status. A UN committee of investigation led by Lakhdar Brahimi concluded in July 2008 that the change in attitude towards humanitarians in some wars had not yet got through to the humanitarian community. The committee paid particular attention to the safety of the staffs of UN humanitarian organizations. 'We continue to think of ourselves as good guys, and just because you have the flag, wherever you go you will be all right,' Brahimi said. 'We need to realize that our flag is not enough protection.'

On one of the fronts in the War on Terror, in Iraq, the message certainly did get through. In August 2003 the UN headquarters in Baghdad was the target of an attack that claimed twenty-two lives, including that of UN Special Representative Sergio Vieira de Mello. In the months that followed, almost all Western aid organizations left Iraq. Since then they have directed their aid projects from Amman, capital of neighbouring Jordan, and even there only a handful risk displaying their logos.

Between 2001, when the War on Terror began, and 2008, more than sixty donor governments allocated a total of over $15 billion to aid for Afghanistan, but exactly where the money ended up is unclear. Neither the donors nor their INGOs dare to visit the projects they finance. The result is an unfathomable channelling of aid billions that is highly susceptible to fraud. [7]

Clinics never actually built, girls' schools where in practice only boys are taught – everyone in Afghanistan can give examples of aid projects that have been financed but not realized. The majority of Western INGOs never venture outside Kabul. Instead they subcontract local and other international NGOs to implement their projects, who in turn engage further subcontractors. A total of four intermediate organizations is common; seven or more is no exception. Each one creams off a proportion of the money allocated. Steadily seeping away, project finance passes from hand to hand until finally someone somewhere in the country gets down to bricklaying, carpentry or ploughing. In the intervening stages, effective supervision of budgets becomes impossible, or is made impossible.

Corp Watch, an independent research institute that investigates and exposes corporate fraud and corruption around the world, eventually managed to trace what had happened to the $15 million USAID had earmarked for the building of a road from Kabul to Kandahar in the south. The money turned out to have been transferred from USAID, via the UN, to an American company that hired a Turkish road-builder. Each intermediate layer absorbed between 6 and 20 per cent of the project funding, so that in the end only cheap, inferior materials could be purchased. According to Corp Watch the stretch of tarmac that resulted was barely any improvement on the unsealed road it replaced, and without annual maintenance it would become impassable within five years. But road maintenance is an expense the Afghan government cannot afford and one for which donors to the project had not allocated funds.

Another example was given by Clare Lockhart, adviser to the United Nations in Afghanistan from 2001 to 2005. She investigated a house-building project in Bamiyan Province. It began in the summer of 2002 with $150 million in the kitty. First the money was transferred by donor governments to an aid agency in Geneva, which allocated 20 per cent to its own organization and then handed over implementation of the project to an organization in Washington, DC. That agency also kept 20 per cent for itself and passed the job on to another organization. Which kept 20 per cent and subcontracted the task of implementation once more. With the money that was left, the final organization in the sequence bought a consignment of wooden beams in neighbouring Iran. It was delivered to Afghanistan by a transport company owned by the governor of Bamiyan Province for five times the normal freighting fee. When at last the beams arrived in the villages selected to receive the aid, they turned out to be too heavy for the loam walls of Afghan houses. The villagers decided the best thing to do with the timber was to chop it up and use it to fuel their cooking fires.[8]

At any given moment, several thousand aid projects large and small are underway in Afghanistan. Local NGO sub-subcontractors are doing very well out of them. By 2004, 2,325 such organizations had already been registered with the Afghan Ministry of Planning. 'First there was Communism, then Talibanism and now there's NGOism,' Kabulis say.

Less laconic was Jean Mazurelle, former director of the World Bank in Kabul. He estimated that 35–40 per cent of all international aid to Afghanistan is 'wrongly spent'. He told the press agency AFP that 'In Afghanistan the wastage of aid is sky-high: there is real looting going on, mainly by private enterprises. It's a scandal. In the thirty years of my career, I've never seen anything like it.'[9]

When asked, aid workers and donors naturally say they control what happens to the money. Staff at the Dutch embassy, for example, through whose hands tens of millions of euros have poured into Afghanistan every year since 2001, assure me that they demand to see receipts or photographs from projects in 'areas that are difficult to access', just as other donors do. 'It's possible that some Dutch money leaks away, but in practice very little. We have the feeling we can rest assured,' a diplomat says.

One Afghan accountant working for USAID has a very different feeling. She carries out spot checks on the effectiveness of such control methods, which USAID uses as well, and she shrugs. 'I can tell one Afghan's handwriting from another's, but foreigners only see squiggles and dots. Sometimes I'm shown a hundred and fifty receipts with the same signature.' And photographs of USAID projects? 'I sometimes see pictures of exactly the same project with different donors. Aid groups are happy to be financed three times over. After all, the donors don't come and look.'

The situation has acquired a nickname in Kabul. The systematic lack of control of aid funding is called 'Afghaniscam'. Afghan racketeers can rake off aid money unhindered, and in areas where the Taliban has regained control, their fighters are able to use unsupervised aid funding to strengthen and expand their popular support.

The more Taliban, the greater the fear among foreigners in Afghanistan. Their security has probably become more expensive than the aid projects they run. Most humanitarians and diplomats in Kabul have withdrawn to their own Forbidden City, the exclusive neighbourhood of Wazir Akbar Khan, where Kabul's rich and famous once lived. To get there you have to pass barricades of piled-up sandbags with armed guards stationed behind them. For the American, British, Australian and South African security companies in Afghanistan, business is booming. They have no trouble recruiting enough personnel to serve all their clients. It's far from unusual for discharged American and NATO soldiers, instead of going home, to get themselves on to the payroll of companies such as Blackwater, DynCorp and USPI. They can easily earn \$1,000 a day, largely tax-free. Local recruits are plentiful too. There's no shortage of warlords and militiamen walking about in Afghanistan who could use the extra income. The American Defense Department now has more contracted employees than troops in the country. An American Congressional Research Service report dated September 2009 said that as of March that year, 52,333 uniformed US military personnel and 68,200 contractors were deployed there. This represents the highest recorded percentage of contractors used in any conflict in the history of the United States. About 16 per cent of them are involved in providing security.[10]

Security companies working for private clients also import as much weaponry as they see fit and do whatever deals they like with local drug dealers and war mafias, or indeed engage in fire-fights with them. They tear around the country in bullet-proof Land Cruisers with tinted windows and no number plates. Anyone getting too close may find the car door flies open and a Western wildman points a machine-gun at him yelling, 'Fuck off or I'll shoot!'

If a client wants to get from A to B, security personnel close off streets or even whole neighbourhoods at will. Taxis, vendors with their watermelons, turkeys, blankets, pots and pans, parakeets in bamboo cages and carpets on their heads, ox carts, wheelbarrows, bicycles and mopeds, beggars sitting on wheeled boards and women in dirty burkas begging for money all simply have to find another way to get to where they are going.

In 2006 Afghan president Hamid Karzai – by that point under the protection of private foreign bodyguards himself – demanded that all private roadblocks in Kabul be dismantled. He was ignored. Most of the security companies hadn't even bothered to ask the appropriate Afghan ministry for work permits, as the law obliges them to do on arrival.

Anyone who gets too close to their clients is sworn at and shoved aside, and the security guys never talk to journalists. So I and a couple of colleagues have little choice but to eavesdrop on them. At a diner near Flower Street in Kabul we creep, plates and all, as close as we can get to the table where a team of American musclemen are eating. They talk about football, the knobs on the dashboards of armoured vehicles and babes and bitches, then about the best way to spend an evening in Kabul. The answer that wins the most votes runs: 'Go to a strip joint, get drunk and then shoot Afghans.' They finish their glasses of beer, squeeze themselves into not one but two bullet-proof vests apiece and tear off through the gates in their Land Cruisers.

The strip joint they were talking about must be one of an estimated eighty brothels in Kabul where the security men, and other members of the reconstruction community in the city, can amuse themselves with pole-dancing Russians and purring, bite-sized Filipinas.

Large areas of the city look just as they did when the Taliban left: ruined and abandoned. The foreigners make things as pleasant for themselves as they can. A reporter for the *New York Times* described how the first of the contracted staff to arrive in town immediately furnished one hotel with a blackjack lounge. A short distance away, British entrepreneurs opened Afghanistan's first cocktail bar, where the hired hands could drink margaritas and Tora Bora Specials at $10 a pop. In a Thai restaurant nearby, chicken curry was soon being served by waitresses flown in from Bangkok, dressed in mini-skirts split to the tops of their thighs, with toy guns tucked into their garters.

For the foreigners, generators hum day and night. As for the rest of the population of Kabul, seven years after the reconstruction operation began only 2 per cent are supplied with electricity. The Westerners have DVDs and laptops. The latest Harry Potter was available in Kabul as quickly as in the 'normal' world; copies of *Harry Potter and the Deathly Hallows* arrived on the plane from Dubai only a few hours after they rolled off the presses in London.

Foreigners can enjoy imported snacks in Chinese, Indian, French, Mexican, American, German, Australian or Nepalese restaurants and eat mega-steaks in the Red Hot 'n' Sizzling, popular with the staffs of the large American firms of contractors that USAID hires to help with reconstruction. They can drink double cappuccinos and smoothies in cosy cafés, slurp foam in a German Beer Garden and dance the salsa at La Cantina. The trendiest club of all is L'Atmosphere, owned by a Frenchman. Humanitarians can be found there with cocktails and glasses of wine, or relaxing in the swimming pool near the bar.

In the air-conditioned shopping mall and in a number of five-star hotels in the city, foreigners can ride lifts and escalators, use their credit cards to withdraw dollars from cash machines, and buy gold jewellery. The malls, restaurants, dance clubs and hotels all have to be guarded by the security companies, of course.

There are several aid projects that may well come to fruition, but for now Afghans complain that their city is still a heap of rubble, their children are hungry, and the schools and hospitals are over-crowded. They complain about the high rents they pay for houses and about the prices of food and fuel, which have shot up. You even hear people sigh that in retrospect life under the Taliban wasn't so bad. At least there weren't any foreigners stealing billions of aid dollars from the people, they say. But even Afghans who feel no nostalgia at all for the Taliban era are angry, because the failing aid operation fosters sympathy for the Taliban among other angry Afghans. Either way, the Taliban is steadily gaining strength.

For one of its biggest attacks yet on the reviled 'force multipliers' of the American and European occupying armies, the Taliban chose to target the elegant five-star Kabul Serena Hotel. With glass and gold trim, saunas, massages, Western food and rooms costing up to

$1,200 a night, the hotel's own website described it as an 'oasis of luxury in a war-ravaged city'. It's much in demand – for the meetings and dinners held by diplomats and donors, for instance. On 14 January 2008 attackers stormed the hotel lobby, straight through the security cordon. On their way to the gym they mowed down eight people, mostly Afghan employees of a security company. An American on a treadmill caught a bullet in the face.

After the massacre at the Kabul Serena, roadblocks became even more numerous, walls even higher, coils of razor wire thicker, security guards more numerous and the Afghans even more angry. Partly because of the repugnance it feels for its occupiers, Afghanistan finds itself in a terrible vicious circle. Unsupervised aid invites theft and corruption, which strengthens and multiplies Taliban support, leading to greater insecurity, which brings more security companies, prompting even more hostility towards foreigners, with greater insecurity, because more Taliban, as a result. So even more aid remains unsupervised.

The circle is complete. In the Afghan tangle, everything is bound up with everything else.

Travelling around is becoming more and more dangerous, so humanitarian organizations increasingly engage in 'management by remote control', or 'long-arm programming', meaning they remain in the safety of their offices in the capital and send local employees out into the field. They assume that local staff and local partner organizations face fewer risks than expats. This assumption is incorrect. From the point of view of the Taliban, local employees of INGOs are collaborators and a legitimate target. The murder of five staff working for Dutch MSF in June 2004 caused a stir, but since then dozens of Afghan INGO workers, including doctors, technicians and mine-clearance experts, have been killed or kidnapped. Convoys of humanitarian aid supplies are ambushed. The local drivers are killed, or have their noses and ears cut off. An Afghan employee of an NGO called Compassion for Human Beings was found dead with a letter pinned to his chest saying he deserved to go to hell because he was cooperating with the Americans. The election of Obama as Bush's successor gave the Taliban no reason to think any differently. Obama's Secretary of State Hillary Rodham Clinton simply continued Bush's aid policy. 'I believe in development, and I believe with all my heart that it truly is an equal partner, along with defense and diplomacy, in the furtherance of America's national security,' she said after she was appointed, in a speech to USAID staff.[11]

Eighty per cent of all victims of violence, fatal or not, among the staffs of Western aid organizations in war zones are residents of the country in question. There is barely any discussion of the ethics of this in the humanitarian world.

Dutch aid workers leaving for a conflict zone are generally briefed on the security situation there and may be taken through exercises involving simulated kidnaps. Local aid workers hardly ever receive this kind of training. The Dutch organization ICCO started giving security training to its local partner organizations in Afghanistan in 2008. It was the first to do so.

'What can a Westerner teach local aid workers about security?' Dutch daily *de Volkskrant* asked security trainer Tom Brabers, an ex-soldier and director of the Centre for Safety and Development (CSD). His answer: 'Scenario thinking. What's the first thing you do when you receive a report of a kidnap? Who should make the decisions during the negotiations? I don't give any answers to questions; I help them shape their thoughts into a security plan.'[12]

Clients of aid organizations are targets as well. An aid project more innocent than a nursery school is hard to imagine, yet hundreds of nursery schools in Afghanistan and Iraq paid for with Western aid money have been forced to close and dozens have been burned to the ground, some with the teachers still in them. 'If you care about your safety in this world and the next, don't send your children to schools financed by infidels,' the Taliban warns in letters to residents of villages and towns that are receiving aid. The 'infidels' are donor governments.

Just as they do little, if anything, to keep their local employees safe, INGOs do little to reduce the risks for aid recipients. Here again 'neutral' apparently means standing aside and saying: this has nothing to do with me, it has to be solved by politicians, or the police.

'Reconstruction troops' who run aid projects in Iraq and Afghanistan pursue what's known as a 'hearts and minds' strategy. It's sometimes called 'Phase Zero of warfare'. Soldiers entering Afghan or Iraqi villages distribute small gifts, ranging from sweets and chewing gum scattered from tank turrets to first-aid kits for impoverished clinics, new roofs for damaged schools, materials for well-digging or repairs to bridges and roads.

During the first American air strikes on the Taliban in Afghanistan in October 2001, a month after 9/11, American warplanes dropped not only bombs but aid packages containing, among other things, pots of peanut butter and American flags. When that turned out to be insufficient – the Taliban didn't lose its following from one day to the next – President George W. Bush promulgated an order via USAID: in future all American aid supplies to Afghanistan were to be clearly stamped 'Gift from the USA'. Secretary of State Powell explained: 'What it does in the Muslim world, is giving an opportunity to see American generosity, American values in action.'

The Dutch NATO soldiers who moved into northern Afghanistan after the American air strikes had €50,000 from the Dutch government to spend on hearts and minds fripperies like school textbooks, the pepping up of a few parched soccer pitches, or repairs to local orphanages. To this day, US army and NATO Provincial Reconstruction Teams (PRTs) moving around in Afghanistan have assets like health care and water pumps on offer, as part of an attempt to win local hearts and minds.

Whether the hearts and minds approach pays off and whether the gifts end up with the people or via the people with Taliban leaders, no one knows. Thirteen donor governments that belong to the military coalition in Afghanistan finance hundreds of hearts and minds projects, but 'in the interests of security' their defence ministries make it virtually impossible for anyone to inspect the books. Nobel Prize-winning economist Joseph Stiglitz investigated Pentagon spending as far as he could and decided that the Pentagon's bookkeeping is 'based on an accounting system inaccurate for anything larger than a grocery store'. The US pays out $16 billion a month to cover the ongoing costs of its military operations in Iraq and Afghanistan, including hearts and minds activities, but 'large amounts of cash go missing', Stiglitz wrote. 'The Department of Defense has failed every official audit of the past 10 years.'[13]

Spending by other coalition governments that engage in hearts and minds operations in the War on Terror is similarly shrouded in secrecy. The Dutch army in the Afghan province of Uruzgan, for instance, runs 'under-the-radar projects' invisible to the Taliban, because villages that accept money from Dutch soldiers without Taliban permission can expect retaliation. They are equally invisible to anyone wanting to check the money is being properly spent.

10. The logic of the humanitarian era

Occasionally, I have thought the worst place for a hungry child to live in Africa today is a country that is at peace with its neighbours and relatively stable. Funding levels rise with the incidence of violence and media interest . . .

James Morris, Executive Director of World Food Programme[1]

'Let me be clear,' said former Secretary-General of the United Nations Kofi Annan in 2004. 'The aid we give them is not charity, it is their right.'[2] He was trying to persuade the rich member states to make a total of $3 billion available to the UN that year to enable it to mount operations in the twenty-one poorest countries in the world. Forty-five million people were waiting to be saved from death by starvation and disease. Only a fraction of the amount came in, because receiving aid is not a right, as Kofi Annan suggested it was – any more than giving aid is a duty. Aid is a favour, which donors grant when it suits them. At any given moment the populations of fifty to sixty countries in the world are afflicted by war, often civil war – in 2008 the figure was sixty-one – but the crisis caravan moves off whenever and wherever it sees fit, scattering aid like confetti. In some countries, the donor darlings, it buckets down, while others, the donor orphans, have to make do with the odd snippet. Or with nothing, because donors – like aid organizations – are free to ignore a crisis. Doing nothing is in fact more the rule than the exception. 'Aid is a lottery,' said Jan Egeland, until 2007 Undersecretary-General for Humanitarian Affairs at the UN. 'You have twenty-five equally desperate communities taking part in this lottery for attention every week. Twenty-four lose and one wins.'[3]

★

Sometimes a couple of kilometres are all that separates donor darlings from donor orphans. During the genocide of April 1994 and the months that followed, the Tutsis in Rwanda received next to nothing from any donor government. All the international money and attention went to the Rwandan Hutus in the camps in Goma a few kilometres away. Lieutenant-General Roméo Dallaire, commander of the small UN force serving in Rwanda at the time, described in his book *Shake Hands with the Devil* the reasons why aid had been sorely needed:

Water was not potable as the waterworks had long since been sabotaged. The creeks and rivers that flowed into Kigali didn't bear thinking about [because corpses were floating in them]. Food was scarce. All over Rwanda crops had rotted in the fields because no one was left to harvest them and bring them to the market. There was no fuel, no electricity, no telephone, or other communications – the lists of nothings increased by the day.[4]

Rotting corpses were still lying above ground months after the genocide, while on the other side of the border-posts, in Goma, carts criss-crossed the UNHCR camps for Hutu *génocidaires* twice a week, providing a regular waste-collection service. 'Even as millions in humanitarian aid flowed into Goma we could not get a few thousand dollars to help in Kigali,' Dallaire wrote. 'We [Dallaire and his UN soldiers] helped anyway, digging into our own pockets when we could, embarrassed that we couldn't do more.' When international donors and aid organizations finally started to become interested in the situation inside Rwanda, Dallaire was barely able to muster any gratitude.

On a daily basis, delegations of politicians, bureaucrats, celebrities, actors, singers, any Tom, Dick or Harry who could manage it, came to Rwanda requesting that we coordinate their visit, their accommodations, their transportation and their itineraries. [. . .] The

one humorous aspect of these visits was that I would make a point
of inviting our distinguished guests to a supper of expired military
rations. Maybe it was adolescent of me, but I truly enjoyed the
amazed looks on people's faces at the sight of these 'state' dinners,
along with their pained gulps as they attempted to eat the hideous
fare that had been our staple for months.[5]

In the lottery to win favour with donors and aid organizations,
victims have to find a way to distinguish themselves from rival
victims. Some hire professionals to draw attention to their cause,
like Colonel Ojukwu of Biafra, who – remarkably cleverly for the
1960s – called in the assistance of a Genevan PR company, or the
Palestinians, who employ press officers. Other groups draw upon
their own experience. They've had more than half a century to
study and test the mechanisms that prompt the Western aid world
to act. Victims' groups are increasingly likely to have a highly
developed understanding of how the humanitarian aid world
works: even people in countries at war have access to the internet.
Most refugee camps have televisions that can pick up CNN, so
refugees see how 'we' portray victims. They learn to fit the expected
image. 'The premise is that Africans lack the capacity to save
themselves and must rely upon the kindness of strangers,' said
President Mbeki of South Africa. 'Conscious or unconscious, this
assumption pervades discourse on Africa. We can argue about who
is to blame for that perception – and we Africans are far from
blameless.'[6]

Groups hoping for aid see that crises can be crossed off the donors'
priority lists after a meeting or two in a Western capital. Or they
learn that another group of victims will have to make do in future
with half the donations it's currently receiving or less. In February
2006, for instance, the World Food Programme asked donors to make
up a shortfall of $220 million so that it could supply sufficient rations
to all its clients until the end of the year. In vain. Instead of the
2,100 calories a day they needed to stay alive and in good health,
20,000 Angolan and 57,000 Congolese refugees suddenly found

themselves with half that amount. Soon underfed children could be seen tottering through the camps, people were surviving by eating leaves from bushes and trees, and refugees were leaving the camps to beg or steal in nearby villages. In 2007 the same fate befell 400,000 refugees in Tanzania. Donors switched their attention to other 'humanitarian territories' and the daily allowance per refugee was cut by a third. In southern Chad at around the same time, food supplies for refugees from Central Africa were reduced, and of the 44,000 Liberian refugees in Sierra Leone, fewer than 2,000, the 'especially vulnerable', received their full rations.

The choice as to which refugees will have to go on a diet is made not by the WFP but by its donors. Seventy to 80 per cent of donations to the WFP come with precise donor instructions about where rations are to be distributed and where not. The head of the WFP, James Morris, explained that donors select countries and regions where they have political interests, or places thought of as high profile that offer a fair chance of positive publicity. 'Ninety per cent of the people who die of hunger and malnutrition don't die in a high-profile situation. In our view there are few phenomena in modern life as political as humanitarian aid,' he said.[7]

John Graham of Save the Children UK described a similar law of humanitarianism: 'If you don't have starving babies you don't get the money.'[8]

Suffering in silence gets you nowhere, as the recipients have learned. Africans especially have to kick up a considerable fuss to be heard and seen by donors, since modern history sets a high threshold for attention to 'yet another African war drama'.

In 2004 less than a quarter of Official Development Assistance was given to the poorest countries. Most went to the front-line states in the War on Terror. Other winners that year included the tsunami victims, with an average of $1,200 per inhabitant of the affected areas. The losers were Congo, with ten aid dollars per head of population (estimated number of dead in the region since the 1990s: 5 million), and the victims of famine in Namibia, with nothing. 'We've received nothing. Not one cent,' said Christiane Berthiaume, spokeswoman for the WFP. 'This is sad, because Namibia is a country that rarely asks for international aid.'[9]

It's 2001 and the announcement that war-torn Sierra Leone has once again been named the world's poorest country by the UNDP is the occasion for a festive gathering in Freetown. Poorest countries are eligible for special international aid programmes. The cream of Freetown society has gathered to toast the decision in a conference room at a recently opened luxury hotel, the property of a Chinese investor. The vice-president hands a copy of the UNDP report to his president, 'Pa' Kabbah, who waves it triumphantly above his head for the photographers. Nice hotel this, the vice-president says. 'But we mustn't have any more of this standard. It gives foreigners the wrong idea. They'll start thinking we're a country of comfort and luxury. Marble floors and gold-coloured bells on reception desks don't do our cause any good.' The guests nod in agreement.

Further along the same Freetown road, by the beach, is the Mamy Yoko Hotel, currently serving as the headquarters of the UN mission in Sierra Leone. It's lunch-break time in the negotiations between the rebel movement, the Revolutionary United Front (RUF), and donor governments. The talks concern the conditions under which the RUF is prepared to lay down its arms. The rebels are stretching their legs, and behind pillars I can see representatives of the EC and the World Bank working their mobile phones.

The RUF delegation seems to consist entirely of wiry teenagers. A month or so ago they were still prowling the bush. Now they stroll in oversized, perhaps borrowed, Western suits to the UN dining room, chatting relaxedly. The buffet is ready. Now and then they slap each other on the back and laugh loudly, the way they've seen important international functionaries do on television.

The coastal strip, a quarter of the country, has been liberated from the rebels and is under the control of UN blue helmets. The remaining three-quarters of Sierra Leone, a region of jungle and diamonds, will be left in the hands of at least four warring parties until an accord has been signed. Today negotiations are underway with the rebels of the RUF. The international peace negotiators are more than prepared to meet RUF demands, since donor governments want to see results. RUF prisoners will be released, RUF negotiators have been lent a plane to carry them to each new round of talks, and there's a demobilization programme for rebel fighters. Anyone handing in a weapon to the UN blue helmets gets $300, board and lodging in a UN reception camp, and training as a mechanic, barber or tailor. Five thousand blue helmets from Nepal and Pakistan are waiting to take over from the rebels in the bush.

During the war the RUF seized the bush town of Makeni and made it their capital. From Freetown in government-held territory the town became as good as unreachable. For years to come, local people gathering firewood in the tropical shrubbery along the road that leads there will stumble over the bodywork of cars and trucks ambushed by rebels and torched. And over the remains of the people they killed in the process. Rebels still control the road, but since the peace negotiations at the Mamy Yoko Hotel began, the terror has been limited to 'tax collection' at a total of forty-two RUF roadblocks.

We judder on like a superball through and around holes in the tarmac. On the roof of the old Opel Kadett that serves as our taxi rocks a metre-and-a-half-high tower of sacks of rice and jerrycans filled with palm oil, a colourful, indignant-looking chicken tethered on top.

Twelve of us sit crammed together inside. Another two passengers ride behind the open lid of the car boot and one lies flat across the bonnet, firmly gripping the broken aerial and the windowless front door.

The mood is excellent. The passengers are glad that this journey is possible again after ten years of war. Our radiator keeps boiling dry, but that's actually a bonus: while the driver goes off with a bucket to look for the nearest stream, we stretch our legs.

High above us three white UN helicopters are on their way to Makeni. 'It's nearly peacetime,' say the passengers with satisfaction.

The closer we get to Makeni, the merrier they all become.

'I know a joke!' one calls out from the front seat. 'What can man see that God never can?' We think for a long time and give up.

'His superior!' the passenger cries out in triumph. We scream with delight at such wit.

Not even the sight of the charred remains of timber and small piles of brick that mark the site of a burned-out village can dampen our spirits. On a wall that escaped the attack we can make out a painting: a couple entwined in a dance. The words 'We Protect Ourselves Against AIDS' are painted below the image.

'They don begin use condom, then di rebel them come kill 'em!' someone calls out from the front seat. Again we shriek with laughter.

One more boiling-radiator stop and a flat tyre later we shamble into Makeni.

Along the sidelines of the town's bald soccer pitch, one row of wooden stands remains. Today they're full of singing and surging rebels, with here and there an uncomfortable-looking white person squashed between them. I recognize the Sierra Leone representative of UNICEF and his counterpart from the World Bank. They must have been in the helicopters we saw whirring this way. The 'Rap Hip Hop Megastar' worshipped in Freetown, Jimmy B, has been flown in too. To give a positive boost to the peace and reconciliation process, the UN has hired the hit musician to hold a Peace Concert. He's protected from the audience by coils of barbed wire and by blue helmets with rocket launchers on their shoulders.

Thick clouds of marijuana smoke drift across the pitch; the rebels are having a ball. General Cut-Throat, Superman, Kill-Man-No-Blood, Gullit, Major Roadblock, Sergeant Satan, Captain Blood Sucker, Colonel Kaka, Sergeant Rape Star and Colonel Saddam: the entire government of the Makeni district seems to have stepped out on to the pitch. In stolen leather coats that reach to the ground, with sunglasses, gold chains round their necks and Nikes with air cushions several centimetres thick, they're break-dancing. Some carry rhesus monkeys on their shoulders, trembling with nerves, and one moonwalks between the blue helmets with a baby chimpanzee on his back like a living rucksack.

'They'll have killed the mother chimpanzee,' a UN soldier from Ghana volunteers gloomily.

'Or they'll have forced the baby chimpanzee to amputate its own mother's arm and then taken the poor creature prisoner and conscripted it,' a fellow soldier opines. That's what the RUF did to human children.

Several of the RUF high command were born in Makeni. They ordered their troops not to destroy the town. Most of Makeni has escaped being burned down or demolished, unlike the rest of the country, but it has been looted and terrorized. The majority of the original population has fled to camps for displaced persons in Freetown.

'RUF Humanitarian Dept. Zone 4' is daubed on one house. Next to it: 'West Side Niggers Don't Play With Us God Is With Us'. A warning to the government in Freetown perhaps. The capital lies to the west of Makeni. With the peace negotiations up and running, rebel commanders have gone right ahead and divided the town up between them into 'humanitarian zones'. In shabby abandoned buildings they've each opened their own 'RUF Humanitarian Headquarters' and appointed themselves 'humanitarian officers', in which capacity they're hoping shortly to receive the promised millions in international aid. Ready and waiting, they sit on beer crates and rickety stools in their humanitarian head offices.

'The whitemen are soon gonna need drivers, security guards and houses. We're gonna provide them,' Colonel Vandamme says eagerly. He has a school exercise book on his lap in which he writes down the rules he's thought up so far for the aid workers.

'Them NGO wifes done reach already for come count how much sick and pikin [children] de na di area.' The rebels call aid workers 'wives' because they care for people. 'I told them they couldn't just

come here and do that. They're my pikin and my sick. Anyone who
wants to count them has to pay me first.'

Two hundred thousand dead in ten years of civil war, hundreds of
thousands wounded or deliberately maimed, half the population
of over 4 million displaced or in exile, hundreds of villages and
towns burned to the ground. Not a single telegraph pole in the
country has been left standing and there's hardly a bridge that hasn't
been dynamited. The war has gone down as the cruellest and most
destructive in the modern history of West Africa. Many experts
dismiss the warriors in Sierra Leone's bush as drug-fuelled maniacs,
but some suspect that a rational, calculated strategy lay behind their
destructive frenzy and thirst for blood – they suggest it was a
deliberate attempt to drive up the price of peace.

I set off to ask RUF leader Mike Lamin whether this is true. I
know I must be somewhere near his house in Makeni when I find
myself having to pick my way between an increasing number of
angrily glaring boys. They hang around in large groups outside
houses and sit in many-headed tangles on the bonnets of parked
cars. The international peace negotiators have given the RUF
leadership vehicles to get them to the various rounds of peace
talks.

Lamin's house, with flaking whitewashed walls and a corrugated-
iron roof, is in a short, dusty street. The rebel leader appears in a
purple shirt and a matching cap with a swishing yellow tassel. Even
indoors his eyes are hidden behind fighter-pilot sunglasses. He nods
towards a new sofa, still wrapped in plastic.

'Hot chocolate?' he asks once I'm sitting down. I daren't say no:
bulky, highly unfavourable reports have been published by human
rights groups about Lamin's men. He snaps his fingers. A servant
brings us two steaming mugs of Nestlé.

'Meat sandwich?' Lamin asks.

'Sounds good,' I answer.

The kitchen rebel comes back with a white loaf and a tin of Spam.
Mike Lamin wields the knife himself. There's no fresh meat left in

Makeni. There's nothing fresh left at all. The RUF has eaten everything. First they consumed all the cattle for kilometres around, then the entire harvest, then the seed grain that should have produced the next harvest. After that, tins were pretty much all that was left.

In the 1999 peace negotiations in the Togolese capital, Lomé, Mike Lamin demanded the post of Minister of Trade and Industry in the government that was to be formed. He became a rebel again when the Lomé Accord was ditched a few months later. The RUF had felt cheated, Lamin explains. 'We'd worked harder than anyone for peace, but we got almost nothing in return.'

For ten years the RUF had fought the Sierra Leone government. 'But you people looked the other way all those years,' says Lamin reproachfully. I prick up my ears. What did he mean by 'you people'?

'What should "we" have done then?' I pronounce the word 'we' as ironically as I can with a mouth full of Spam. 'It wasn't *our* war, was it? Sierra Leoneans started it, Sierra Leoneans could have stopped it.'

'There was nothing to stop for,' says Lamin. 'Everything was broken and you people weren't here to fix it. All you cared about was the whiteman's war in Yugoslavia and the camps in Goma. You just let us go on fighting.'

The RUF leadership eventually managed to break the cycle and save the country from total annihilation, Lamin explains. By using more and more violence, the RUF forced the Sierra Leone government army to use more and more violence too. 'And then even more. And even more still.' Mike Lamin continues: 'It was only when you saw ever more amputees that you started paying attention to our fate.'

The peace negotiations in Lomé were the result. The international community promised a reconstruction operation if the parties would sign an accord, exactly as the RUF had planned, Lamin says. But President 'Pa' Kabbah cunningly made off with the RUF success. 'He stole all the credit for the "amputee factor",' Lamin grumbles. Kabbah came to Lomé clutching an adorable little three-year-old toddler, a girl with only one arm. The other arm had been hacked off by the RUF, Kabbah said, in front of camera teams from the international media. 'For this girl, I sign this peace,' he declared. And so the RUF got the *blame* for the amputations, instead of the respect it deserved for saving the country by boosting the production of amputees. 'Without the amputee factor you people wouldn't have come,' Lamin is convinced. Kabbah became a donor darling and the RUF received no reward for its pains. Well, all right, the rebels in the person of Mike Lamin were granted the Ministry of Trade and Industry, in a country without either trade or industry. And the vice-president was to be a member of the RUF too, namely Foday Sankoh. But soon after the accord was signed he was arrested on murder charges and thrown into jail.

A year, perhaps eighteen months after Lomé, the RUF broke apart into dissatisfied and extremely dissatisfied factions. In Mamy Yoko one group is still trying to derive a modicum of power from fresh rounds of negotiations, but it's impossible now to turn the ship around. The first 6,000 blue helmets have already landed for what will soon be the biggest UN mission in the world, spearheading the costliest humanitarian aid operation in the world. For years to come, around $300 million annually will be poured into aid projects that directly or indirectly support 'Pa' Kabbah's government. And Mike Lamin is eating Spam out of a tin.

By this stage he's more lying on the sofa than sitting on it. He snaps his fingers again. The kitchen rebel comes trotting up to him with a sloshing jerrycan and two plastic cups.

'Palm wine?' asks Lamin. Through the open window a woman's screeches drift in, along with smacking sounds from the hand that is hitting her.

'Just a drop then,' I say.

When I step muzzily out on to the street an hour later, the angry-looking boys are still hanging around. One of them comes up to me. He waves his maimed hands in my face. I've seen fists like his before in this country. That's how they end up if you shove them into a fire for long enough. They ball up and fuse that way.

I stuff a 1,000-leone note into the boy's trouser pocket, the equivalent of 20 euro cents, and a piece of chewing gum into his mouth.

The international Truth and Reconciliation Commission (TRC) for Sierra Leone, which collected witness statements from hundreds of victims and perpetrators after the war, mentions a gathering of rebels and government army soldiers said to have taken place in the bush in Koinadugu District. It must have been late 1997, early 1998. 'They felt they were not getting enough international recognition and they pointed to how much international coverage the amputations were getting as compared to other aspects of the war,' the TRC report *Witness to Truth* says.[10] Those present are said to have agreed to continue with the amputations for that reason. One witness told the TRC, 'When we started cutting hands, hardly a day BBC would not talk about us.' By 1999 the UN in Freetown was reporting that special amputation squads had been formed. Human Rights Watch interviewed members of 'cut-hands gangs'. One of them said he had received promotion after he brought back a rice bag full of hands.

'Regardless of whether such a meeting [in Koinadugu District] did take place, the notion that the degree of media coverage of amputations influenced the degree of perpetration of this violation [. . .] seems to make sense,' the TRC report observes. 'This seems to be a deranged way of addressing problems, but for a faction [. . .] already vetted in war by several years [. . .] it might be a plausible way of thinking.'

Without violence and devastation, no aid. And the more ghastly the violence and the more complete the devastation the more comprehensive the aid. The logic of the humanitarian era comes home to me with mounting force. A small unit of Nigerian blue helmets is manning an outpost of stacked car tyres at the edge of Makeni. Beyond it lies no man's land, territory held by an RUF faction that is not taking part in the negotiations in Freetown. I want to know whether the rebels there have fathomed the logic out as well.

'Sometimes we see them spying on us from the bushes,' says one of the blue helmets. 'So we beckon them over: "Come here, come on, we've got a demob scheme for you, don't be afraid. You'll get three hundred dollars!" But they feel it's not enough, I think.'

After I've been hanging around for an hour and a half at the Nigerian tyres, unsure of the best way to find an answer, a moped approaches. The enthusiastic rebel riding it is dressed in disintegrating baby-blue overalls and a pair of flip-flops. I clamber on to the back and he gives me what looks like a wok to wear as a helmet. It seems safer than the thing on his own head, which resembles a rice cooker. Before we ride off into the bush he does a few laps of honour around the Nigerian car tyres with me on the luggage rack as his trophy. The blue helmets cheer. Several throw their blue berets festively into the air.

Soon there's no road left to speak of. It's been raining and the path has turned into a rally-car skidpan. We splash through puddles with ducks and toads swimming around in them and on the dry bits we squidge fat millipedes under our tyres. Where the road is impassable we slalom between coconut palms and the bamboo lining the verge.

My journey through the dark side of humanitarian aid operations ends at a nail-spiked plank: a roadblock, manned by a rebel with only one lens in his sunglasses. The moped engine is turned off. From the transistor radio the roadblock rebel is holding I can hear a BBC World Service news broadcast about a NATO operation in Afghanistan.

More rebels appear from burned-out cars near the roadblock, dressed like American West Coast rap artists on MTV. One is wearing Air France headphones, but there's no sign of a Walkman. They stink of stale sweat and they look angry, shake the moped, wave their Kalashnikovs and one or two spears and shout above one another. A rebel sweetheart comes to join in the shouting. She's wearing platform soles and carrying a baby in a kanga on her back.

'This is my country!' someone shrieks.

'Why aren't you in Freetown for the peace talks?' I shout above the shouting.

'Power to us!' one lad yells. For some reason he's wearing a bathing cap.

'If you destroy everything, you'll soon be in power over a garbage dump!' I shout in reply.

'Whitewoman! Do you know what "war" means?' asks the one-lens rebel in a shrill voice.

'Yes. Fighting.' I bite back.

'Wrong! W-A-R means "Waste All Resources". Destroy every-thing. Then you people will come and fix it.'

So sure enough, any old bush version of Ice-T and Snoop Dogg can explain the humanitarian logic to me. If you use enough violence, aid will arrive, and if you use even more violence even more aid will arrive. There's nothing new in this, and the sums involved are getting bigger all the time, but there's never been a coordinated answer from the world of humanitarian aid.

'Yes, but, good grief, should we just do nothing at all then?' asks Max Chevalier of Handicap International when I get back to Freetown.

'Listen,' he goes on. 'A colleague of mine, another physio-therapist, came into my office this morning white as a sheet. A patient had just been to see her, a girl, maybe sixteen years old. Rebels had hacked off her hand and forced her to eat it. Are we supposed to simply walk away and abandon that girl?'

In this humanitarian era we need at the very least to ask that question. Otherwise we'll be storing up even worse things for tomorrow.

Afterword:
Ask them questions

Aid is thus like champagne: in success you deserve it,
in failure you need it.

Development economist Professor Peter Bauer,
London School of Economics[1]

No doubt you'll now want to know how it *ought* to be done.

When a message is painful, we always want a quick, ready-made solution to numb the pain. I don't have *the* solution. Solutions will anyhow vary from case to case. Darfur is not Afghanistan and the RUF rebels in Sierra Leone are not the Hutus in Goma. My argument is that we must stop avoiding the questions and start discussing how to do better.

The discussion is often 'flawed' because it's emotional. The reaction to criticism is all too frequently: 'Oh! Should we simply do nothing at all any more?'

The option of doing nothing must be available, if that would be better, but I'm not arguing for 'doing nothing at all' any more. What I am advocating is that we no longer exempt the system from criticism. Too much is going wrong. It's as if staffing a clinic or a food distribution centre in a distant, poor country in crisis somehow or other brings immunity with it. As far as I'm aware, no aid worker or aid organization has ever been dragged before the courts for failures or mistakes, let alone for complicity in crimes committed by rebels and regimes.

Humanitarians carry the integrity of their Red Cross principles – neutrality, independence and impartiality – before them like a shield, and think it self-evident that the principles are more important than their consequences. Theirs is an ineluctable humanitarian duty, they argue. They have no choice but to ease human suffering, even if the bad guys benefit. Imagine, say the humanitarians: a motorist kills someone and is injured himself, because he was drunk at the wheel. You can't just leave the guy bleeding on the road, can you? He has a right to help, like any other human being.

But the comparison is not valid. In constitutional states like ours you patch up the driver and hand him over to the authorities. The courts will make sure he's locked up so that he doesn't kill anyone else. Aid organizations working in places where such a judicial apparatus doesn't exist, or serves only one party, therefore most certainly are responsible for the consequences of their aid.

The question is not whether we 'should simply do nothing at all, then'. The question is: where does the balance lie, if we weigh up the positive effects of aid against its exploitation by warring parties? At what point do humanitarian principles cease to be ethical?

Humanitarian crises are almost always political crises, or crises for which only a political solution exists. When donors, militias and armies, not least our own national or NATO armies, play politics with humanitarian aid, NGOs cannot afford to be apolitical.

Florence Nightingale and Henri Dunant differed as to how it should be done. The dilemma raises its head time and again – at its ugliest in the Second World War. ICRC cooperation with the Nazi regime in Germany has been called the 'mother of all controversies' in the humanitarian world. The ICRC knew by 1942 that the Holocaust was happening, but at a meeting on 14 October that year the organization decided to keep the information confidential. It felt the evil in the camps was outweighed by the importance of its own principles of neutrality and impartiality. It kept silent, so as not to turn the Nazis against it. A ban on working in Nazi territory might cost lives.

Would the Nazis have abandoned the Holocaust if the ICRC had publicized what was going on? We don't know, but probably not. It's equally unlikely that the Nazis would have shut off ICRC access to victims in occupied areas. Nazi Germany needed the ICRC as much as the other belligerents did, if only for aid to German prisoners of war in Allied hands.

The ICRC now calls that decision to remain silent a 'tragic mistake'. Since then, the humanitarian aid industry has made the same tragic mistake several times. In Ethiopia in the 1980s, aid organizations helpfully provided the regime with money and supplies during a forced migration programme that cost tens of thousands of people their lives. In Goma in the 1990s humanitarian organizations helped the Rwandan *génocidaires* to regroup, enabling them to continue their extermination campaign against the Tutsis in Rwanda. In Darfur, aid agencies are paying millions of euros in taxes to a regime accused under international law of the mass murder of a segment of its own people. Again and again, dictators and rebel leaders turn the international aid industry into what the Nazis made the ICRC: involuntary collaborators. The humanitarians don't opt for a refusal to collaborate. There are no rules or agreements about ethical boundaries, and NGOs make decisions about where to work based not primarily on ethical considerations but on the availability of donor contracts.

Besides, each aid organization specializes in its own small task within large aid operations. They don't feel they are part of a whole. They look at themselves and think: other organizations may get it wrong, but we're different. In response to the publication of this book in the Netherlands, Dutch aid agencies hastened to point their fingers at the 'international community' and its failings, and at a 'lack of political will' to solve hunger and conflict. But they have a responsibility of their own. Aid organizations are part of a huge international aid industry and the reality is that they operate in a world that lacks the political will to avert crises. So what conclusions do NGOs come to about their role? Where do they draw the line?

It seems as if the debate within the aid world is tremendously lively and critical. After every international aid campaign, organizations promise to 'learn lessons' and to implement 'improvements', and they point to 'a degree of progress'. But the debate goes round in circles.

After the débâcle in Goma, 400 aid organizations from eighty countries came together in what they called the Sphere Project, to create a shared handbook of agreed standards. It sets out the minimum that NGOs in disaster areas ought to achieve.[2] It contains recommendations, not enforceable rules.

At around the same time, in 1997, a number of major INGOs created the Active Learning Network for Accountability and Performance in Humanitarian Action (ALNAP) to exchange the latest ideas on accountability. ALNAP puts out a regular publication called *Review of Humanitarian Action*. The seventh issue, dated May 2008 (more than ten years after the founding of Sphere and ALNAP), concludes: 'The humanitarian system still lacks a systematic and regular means of assessing its overall performance. [. . .] There are still no agreed definitions [or] baselines and no mechanism that can track and assess performance.' Its second key conclusion: the humanitarian system would function better if organizations worked collectively instead of operating as competitors in a free market. The predominance of what ALNAP has called a 'me-first mindset' makes aid organizations vulnerable to manipulation and abuse by warring parties. The humanitarian community was already well aware of this during the crisis in Goma, when Hutu extremists exploited competition between the many NGOs that came to help them. The Hutu extremists were able to pursue a strategy of divide and rule. The INGOs were their willing captives. That was in 1994. More than fifteen years later, in 2009, in Darfur, NGOs still find themselves in exactly the same lamentable situation. I am reminded again of what the NGO employee wrote to me from Darfur in 2006: 'It drives me wild that the "humanitarian community" is so spineless in its dealings with the regime. If there was some collective spirit, we might be able to avoid becoming in effect sub-branches of the Sudan state.'

The conclusion is obvious: if the aid industry is left to control itself instead of being controlled, then reforms aren't going to happen any time soon.

Journalism bears responsibility too, but in practice journalists scarcely question aid organizations. They are content to let NGOs guide them around refugee camps, for example. If such a camp were in the Netherlands or the UK and contracted out not to an NGO but to a care company or a catering firm, then journalists would want to know precisely why it was needed, whether in fact it really was needed, how much money was being raked off and by whom, whether the aid workers had the proper diplomas for aid work, whether they were paying due attention to the rights of residents, to neighbours and to the environment, what kind of aftercare the care companies intended to provide and whether or not local authorities were sharing the benefits. But when it comes to aid agencies, journalists automatically approve. Aid organizations are businesses dressed up like Mother Teresa, but that's not how reporters see them. Few journalists specialize in the aid industry. If the crisis caravan heads for a country in Asia, the Asia correspondent is dispatched to report; if the humanitarians travel to Africa, then 'our man' in Nairobi goes to look at the camps. Often the journalists reporting on an aid campaign are also financed, or at least accommodated, by one of the aid agencies taking part in the caravan.

The public too feels little urgent need to take a critical look, since ultimately emergency humanitarian aid costs us peanuts: the occasional tenner paid into a charity account and some $6 billion a year out of the combined tax revenues of the world's richest countries. Americans, the most generous givers, spend more than twice that amount – $14 billion a year – on cosmetic surgery alone: Botox treatments, liposuction and vaginal corrections. Dutch households tip food worth half as much, €3 billion, into the bin every year.

But to warlords in poor, crisis-stricken countries, the aid billions are anything but peanuts. In some wars aid capital is decisive. Under certain circumstances trading in aid supplies may be the most important economic activity around, and money and goods from

NGOs are weapons in military strategies, including those of our own armies. What responsibilities should we ourselves recognize, as donors to aid operations?

Dare to spoil the atmosphere during national fundraising campaigns: ask the aid workers questions! If they say what they're doing helps, ask who's going to be helped by that food, by those medicines. Innocent victims, warlords, or both? What do aid organizations regard as the maximum acceptable, when it comes to money and supplies that go missing? At what stage does the contribution of an aid operation to the war economy qualify as 'doing harm'?

Two Humanitarian Affairs Advisers for MSF Operational Centre Amsterdam (MSF OCA) point out that the humanitarian community is obliged under international law to ensure it is in full control of its resources and thus minimize contributions to the war economy:

Article 23 of the Geneva Convention IV specifies that: 'A party shall allow free passage of certain goods through its territory [. . .] subject to the condition that this party is satisfied that there are no serious reasons for fearing that:

a) consignments might be diverted from their destinations

b) control might not be effective

c) a definite advantage may accrue to the military efforts or the economy of the party's enemy.'

It follows that, unless an organization can guarantee the above, there is no corresponding obligation on the part of armed actors to provide access for humanitarians to the conflict-affected population. Each organization thus has an obligation to ensure that it is in full control of its resources, including supervision of the distribution of relief items, verification of distribution reports and spot-checks of warehouses.[3]

Find out whether organizations are sufficiently independent to decide just who gets their aid. In war zones, aid workers seldom are.

And have the audacity to ask whether doing something is always better than doing nothing. Saying no certainly is an option. We say no all the time. Most donor governments and private donors give money based on newspaper headlines, not the extent and urgency of human suffering.

If we do decide to pay aid organizations to go somewhere, we should demand they explain exactly what they think they're going to achieve there and how.

If we don't ask these questions for our own benefit, then we should ask them for the sake of the people who'll see our next crisis caravan move in.

Aid speak

'We have to define our position. Where do we stand? Who are we?'

'Well, I think it's more that we have to draw out the issues. I've already clustered them: traditions, women, justice, and knowing what communities want to achieve.'

'We've been screwing around with democracy for ages, but what we're really talking about is participation, of course.'

'But where do we stand then?! We're talking about a specific form of governance, aren't we?'

'Well . . . governance . . . more like local government. That's our thing.'

'Enabling communities to establish relationships through institutions is what I mean. The question is whether the local communities can be brought on board.'

'You know, I reckon decision-making's the main issue, guys.'

'No no no, communities! Because they're vulnerable! Especially women in communities!'

'The more we can involve them in decision-making, the closer we'll get to democratic government.'

'Joint programmes, that's what it's all about!'

'Yes, of course, exactly what I'm saying. Getting together to solve things.'

'A more participatory approach, you mean? Justice and reconciliation and so on? You know, I really wonder how our communities visualize that.'

Table talk between international aid workers in Afghanistan, 2007

'Sometimes it seems as if we're only concerned about the aid world and not about the world,' is how one evaluation report by the international economic development aid organization OECD puts it, with some dismay. The aid world splashes about in murky alphabet soups, wrapping itself in jargon that's often impenetrable to outsiders. Who knows what IFI is? Or ODA? Who even *wants* to know?

Here's a glossary from and about the aid world.

A

Absorptive capacity – The maximum amount of aid money that can usefully be spent in a crisis zone. When many donors and aid organizations descend on a crisis zone simultaneously, the absorptive capacity is often inadequate for their enormous budgets. 'In this country it's simply impossible to think up enough viable projects to spend all our money on,' said a representative of the European Commission in Freetown, Sierra Leone.

Accountability – Traceable spending of donor funds. Aid organizations and donors bring this concept to bear when critics once again accuse them of throwing money at problems and failing to produce results. In the complicated reality of humanitarian aid, accountability doesn't amount to much. Not in relation to individual aid organizations, since the fact the books balance at home says little about the state a project has got into in a far-off country in crisis. Nor in relation to the aid industry as a whole. If aid organizations make evaluations of their expenditure public at all, then they are of little use in drawing conclusions about the industry in general. Most organizations use their own bookkeeping methods, which can't be compared on equal terms.

To increase the illusion of accountability, aid agencies place demands on their partner organizations in distant, impoverished countries and they are not to be trifled with. The projects they finance are showered with conditions, rules and assessment tools, quite apart from the insistence on prompt quarterly reports and other provisional evaluations. All that matters, as ever, is that it all adds up on paper.

Africa – The continent of Africa is made up of fifty-four countries with a total population of 900 million, but most media coverage presents it as one country, hot and dusty, with boundless plains full of nature reserves and refugee camps. The continent is reported either as overpopulated, so people can't grow enough food and starve, or depopulated by AIDS and war. The Africans in these stories rarely dress in suits and ties. Either they carry Kalashnikovs or they're half-naked with prominent ribs and bare breasts. Or it's Nelson Mandela.[1]

'The festering disaster of our age,' said Nobel Prize-winner Henry Kissinger of Africa in the 1970s. Former British prime minister Tony Blair called 1990s Africa 'the scar on the conscience of the world'. And UN food-supply expert Jean Ziegler predicted that in the new millennium Africa would be like a 'raft at sea at night. It is drifting away and is slowly vanishing off the Western world's radar.' Africa is also known as the 'dark continent' and the 'lost continent'. Clearly, Africa has an image problem.

UN studies show that not Africa but the Arab world has the poorest, weakest, most illiterate, underdeveloped, unhealthy, benighted and backward populations on the globe, but whenever even the tormented Iraqis think of misfortune, Africa springs to mind. One resident of Baghdad said of humanitarian aid workers who try to decide what's best for Iraqis: 'What are they thinking of? We're not in Africa. We don't live in trees.'[2]

Some people are *Afro-optimists*. They cling to the idea that Africa can surely be saved, if only the continent is given a fair chance.

Aid Angels – Attractive young ladies employed by aid agencies as spokeswomen. First described by captivated male journalists in their stories from the refugee camps in Goma, ex-Zaire (1994). The Aid Angels contribute to the *halo effect* produced by humanitarian aid agencies.

Aid recipients – Organizations that refer to the recipients of their aid as 'clients' imply that their donor funding is being spent in a businesslike and responsible manner. Organizations that call the recipients 'beneficiaries' imply that anyone selected to receive their aid is being done a tremendous favour – even if in reality that's not the case (see **Phantom aid**).

Aid workers build *aid careers* on the helplessness of aid recipients.

So it's just as well there are *aid addicts,* people and governments suffering from a compulsion to ask for aid again and again. *Professional victims* also keep asking for aid, but in a calculated manner. They engage in *strategic victimhood.*

AIDS – The only disease with its own UN aid organization: UNAIDS. Also known as 'God's judgement' and 'today's bubonic plague'. 'At least as much of a threat to world peace as terrorism,' according to UNAIDS – which makes that organization an adherent of the 'breeding ground theory': AIDS leads to poverty, poverty to frustration and frustration to terrorism.

Organizations that tackle diseases other than AIDS like to latch on to the success of the *AIDS lobby.* SARS aid groups, for example, optimistically attributed an 'AIDS-like potential' to SARS, a lung disease that has now all but vanished.

Autumn remainders – As the end of the year approaches, the quality standards donors apply to aid proposals submitted by NGOs are lowered, since donor budgets have to be spent by 31 December each year.

B

Bono and Bob – Singers Bono and Bob Geldof had a joint audience with Pope John Paul II in 1999 to entreat his support for their campaign for debt relief for poor countries. His Holiness wanted to try on Bono's famous sunglasses. 'If the Catholic Church is the glam rock of religion, this guy was just the most vivid of performers,' an admiring Bono said later in an interview. The two *musical missionaries* believe handing out compliments to world leaders is more effective than criticizing them. Bono therefore praised President George W. Bush as 'passionate and sincere' about tackling Third World poverty, and he called Blair and Gordon Brown (then still Britain's chancellor of the exchequer) 'the Lennon and McCartney of global development'. The two 'pop politicians' are sometimes referred to as the 'bards of Blair and Bush'.

Bono sends *Love Messages* to governments that do the right thing in the fight against poverty. Countries that don't do the right thing are given a *Badge of Shame* by Bob Geldof.

The strategy of praise and prizes has proved its worth. In 2005, when the World Bank was looking for a new leader, Bono was tipped as a candidate. The job went to Paul Wolfowitz, but one of the first people he phoned after his appointment was, sure enough, Bono. Because he's full of good ideas. In the late 1990s the Clinton administration wanted to cancel two-thirds of the $6 billion in debt that the poorest African countries owe the United States. Bono flew to Washington to demand cancellation of 100 per cent. Not just because he thought it was the right thing to do but because 'you can't sing about two-thirds of something. It has to feel like history,' as he said in the *New York Times*. 'Incrementalism leaves the audience in a snooze.'

Meanwhile, Blair thanked Bob Geldof for lobbying on behalf of African famine victims by appointing him a member of the Commission for Africa, a think-tank established by the former British prime minister which helps shape British policy on Africa.

Musical aid campaigns by Bono and Bob Geldof – 'Band Aid', 'Live Aid' and 'Live8' – have been dubbed the 'White Band's Burden', a tongue-in-cheek reference to the 1899 poem 'The White Man's Burden' by Rudyard Kipling, which tells of the solemn duty of colonizers to civilize their conquered native populations ('half-devil and half-child'): 'Take up the White Man's burden / Send forth the best ye breed / Go bind your sons to exile / To serve your captives' need', etc.

When world-famous, mega-rich musicians sing songs for poor people and claim in between numbers that, for instance, poverty on earth can be halved by buying a CD, they are engaging in what's known as *rock-star economics*. Some less *artistic economists* tend to say that world poverty's causes and solutions are a little more complicated, and that calculations like these merely give rulers of poor countries an excuse to sit on their hands.

Film stars and sporting heroes engage in *celebrity activism* too. When they succeed in getting their good causes on television they have a *Bono moment*. The UNHCR sent *goodwill ambassador* Angelina Jolie to refugee camps in Africa with camera teams in tow. Mia Farrow went to visit the Sudanese refugees in Chad for UNICEF. The International Rescue Committee invited George Clooney to go to Darfur, and Brad Pitt visited Save the Children projects in Ethiopia.

The media insist on famous people getting involved, so the offending aid organizations claim. 'The appetite of the press is what drives it,' said a spokeswoman for Oxfam UK. 'We want to get our issues out there and if we are always asked "Who have you got?" we go and find someone.'

C

Civil society – A term often used in project proposals drawn up by aid organizations. Civil society is seen as a counterpart to state institutions. It can refer to almost anything, from neighbourhood cafés and human rights groups all the way to Rotary Clubs, the Pastry Cooks' Union and the charity Send a Cow.

Complex emergency – A situation that involves war, displacement, sickness and hunger simultaneously in one place. Some say it's nothing more than a label aid organizations attach to emergencies 'to cover up the fact that one doesn't know what's going on'.[3]

Contract-hoppers – The generalists of the aid world. They hop from disaster to disaster, aid agency to aid agency, project to project. One minute they're 'taking the war out of the children' in Sierra Leone, the next they're digging latrines at refugee camps in Darfur. 'Is it Thursday? Then this must be Afghanistan,' is the joke told among contract-hoppers.

Corruption – When aid fails, the powerlessness of aid workers and donors in the face of 'corrupt local governments' is often blamed. Africa has a particular reputation in this regard, but according to the Berlin-based research institute Transparency International, Italy is more corrupt than Botswana, Greece more corrupt than South Africa and the situation in Poland worse than in Ghana. Theft of EU funds by EU staff by means of fraudulent development aid contracts in Africa in 1999 was at the heart of a scandal that led to the resignation of the European Commission under the presidency of Jacques Santer.

In June 2005 the European Union's anti-fraud department had to carry out another investigation, this time into thirty-two NGOs based in various EU member states on suspicion of fraud on a grand scale. They'd received EC funding for projects in areas including the Palestinian Territories and the Balkans, then sent out a fresh set of invoices for the same projects to the World Bank and USAID, receiving payment a second time. Brussels refused to make public the names of the organizations involved but was willing to let slip that 'a great deal of money' was involved.

In 2003, in an effort to tackle corruption worldwide, the UN Convention Against Corruption presented a treaty to UN member states. Only twenty-seven of the 191 UN countries, half of them in Africa, were prepared to commit to the treaty. Not a single member of the G7 (see under **G**) signed the convention. Officially this has nothing to do with the fact that the most important G7 member state, the US, is ranked number twelve on the list of most corrupt countries in the world.

Cultural relativism – A common consequence among aid workers of frustration at the lack of results from aid projects. A major symptom is thinking aloud that, compared to white people, black people suffer less, or differently, since they're already so used to pain and discomfort.

D

Debt – The problem of debt faced by poor countries can be traced back in large part to the *relaxed lending climate* of the 1960s and 70s, when rich nations lent money like water. Often to dubious regimes, often in the context of the Cold War, when leaders were rewarded for their dedication to anti-Communism rather than their leadership qualities. Many loans were not used for the purposes intended but found their way into private bank accounts in Switzerland and London. Debts grew year by year as the interest due mounted up.

Contemporary anti-imperialists in particular believe that responsibility for such debts should be shared by Western financial institutions. They point to the example of the IMF, which continued lending money to the Democratic Republic of Congo (then still Zaire) even when it was common knowledge that President Mobutu was siphoning off billions for his own use. Why should the dirt-poor Congolese have to give a third of their tiny incomes to pay off the debts that Mobutu built up? Campaigners argue that countries whose debts were entered into by dictators or other corrupt leaders since ousted should qualify for *debt forgiveness*.

But cancelling debt creates an ethical problem of its own. One leader borrows, invests sensibly and repays the loan; another borrows, throws a party or embarks on a military adventure over the border, can't meet repayments and has the debt cancelled. The *lend and forgive approach* rewards incompetence and punishes good behaviour.

Development goal – 'The true end goal of development is to lead the kind of life there is reason to value.'[4]

Diversion – Euphemism for making aid money and aid supplies disappear. They are 'diverted' to another destination, such as someone's trouser pocket.

Donor accoutrements – 'Pilot studies, feasibility reports, priority definitions, budgetary channels, project application checklists, quarterly reports, evaluation programmes, etc.'[5]

Donor fatigue – Sets in when images of human suffering are shown so often that people grow insensitive, instead of being jolted awake, and tighten their purse strings as a result. To judge by the steady annual rise in aid budgets, donor fatigue is a myth. Indiscriminate targeting of our *charitable instincts* certainly is a factor, however, judging by the number of times a year aid organizations express their *funding blues* by talking about the latest 'forgotten humanitarian disaster'.

Dutch disease – In countries and regions where aid is the only source of income, aid organizations and the UN are the only relevant employers. Sometimes hundreds of local applicants may leap at a single vacancy. Humanitarians hire security guards, drivers, interpreters, gardeners, houseboys, technicians, people with linguistic or administrative skills and professionals. The better educated the staff, the greater a project's chances of success, so aid organizations routinely poach the best people from local trade and industry and from public services. Hospitals in countries in crisis see their doctors, nurses and midwives leave to work on aid projects, and schools find themselves without teachers, who have opted to work for aid organizations, as interpreters for instance. Aid agencies pay them up to twenty times their old salaries. They also 'buy' key civil servants in the countries where they operate by connecting them up with aid projects.

The IMF calls this phenomenon the 'Dutch disease', after the corrosive effect on the Dutch economy of the discovery of major natural gas fields in the 1970s. 'The only proven impact of development aid is its negative influence on the competitive position of the recipient country and the shift of resources and workers, including skilled workers, from the productive sector to the public sector in which aid money is concentrated.'[6]

This happened to Kosovo in 1999, for example. After the NATO bombing campaign, more than 300 humanitarian aid organizations moved into the tiny Yugoslav province with at least €1 billion to spend.

'So many organizations, and they fought for the best-trained local staff. Offering salaries of ten times the amount we could pay, they robbed our hospitals of doctors, our businesses of technicians, our institutions of qualified personnel,' said the director of the Kosovo branch of Mother Teresa's organization Gani Demolli.[7] He saw most of his 1,700 social and medical staff defect to take jobs with foreign organizations and was forced to shut up shop.

The foreigners vanished as suddenly as they came, he said. 'We were left behind stunned and confused, unemployed and without any ideas for the future.'

Aid organizations themselves, and their donors, think back to Kosovo as one of the most successful humanitarian interventions prior to the tsunami.

E

Empowerment – A word that often figures in aid agencies' project proposals, promising that aid money will be spent on 'empowering' the local population so that people don't become, or remain, passive and dependent on aid.

F

Feelgood items – 'The committee funded virtually all of Mr Bush's requests for defense but chopped the money for foreign assistance from $5.6 billion to $3 billion. Most of the trims came from what Republicans called "feelgood" items, including reconstruction and democracy projects for Afghanistan.'[8]

Flag-planting – Ensuring your organization gets to a disaster area as quickly as possible, preferably before anyone else, to lay claim to victims and projects ahead of the competition. The practice of flag-planting makes it seem as if very many aid agencies have sprung into action on behalf of victims in disaster zones, but in fact the flag-planters may still have a long way to go before they can finance and staff their presence.

Flagship projects – Aid projects whose publicity value for donors and aid organizations is more important than, for instance, their usefulness or ethics. Visibility is a chronic, time-consuming problem for aid agencies and donor organizations. A tried and tested tactic is the pumping up of a crisis by means of 'fact inflation'. The highest estimates of the numbers dead, wounded, displaced or at risk of starvation will get into the papers, even if backed by wafer-thin evidence (see **Guesstimates**).

Full belly view – The broader view of the world that a person can have once his or her basic needs are provided for.

F-word, the – Experts and the people involved often quarrel for years after a disaster as to which it was: 'F', meaning famine, or just a shortage of food. The final verdict is a sensitive matter, since neither governments nor aid agencies like to hear themselves mentioned in the same breath as the F-word. It would imply that their efforts at prevention had failed. Semantic eccentricities result (see also **G-word** and 'Why is famine so hard to define?', by Alex Whiting for AlertNet, 16 September 2005).

Is the word 'famine' applicable for instance if food is available in a particular region but only for people with money? Often the problem in a 'famine region' is not a lack of food but the price and distribution of the food available.

This was the case in Niger in 2005. 'In Tahoua market, there is no sign that times are hard. Instead, there are piles of red onions, bundles of glistening spinach, and pumpkins sliced into orange shards. There are plastic bags of rice, pasta and manioc flour, and the sound of butchers' knives whistling as they are sharpened before hacking apart joints of goat and beef. A few minutes' drive from the market, along muddy streets filled with puddles of rainwater, there is the more familiar face of Niger. Under canvas tents, aid workers coax babies with spidery limbs to take sips of milk, or the smallest dabs of high-protein paste,' wrote the *Guardian* on 1 August 2005. The food in Tahoua's market was too expensive for the children's parents to buy.

In late 2003 and early 2004 parts of Niger began to suffer the results of lower rainfall and more locusts than usual, but Niger's harvest was only 11 per cent down on its average for the preceding five years. In the spring of 2004, when the local paper *La Flamme* predicted that 'hunger would knock at the gates' of the affected region, Maradi, and that the malnutrition sickness kwashiorkor was threatening 20,000 children, Niger's merchants saw their chance. They quickly bought up the national grain stocks for CFA 10,000 (€15) per sack. Then they quietly waited for food prices to rise.

By late June a sack of grain was already fetching CFA 30,000 (€46), an historical record for the country. In August aid workers started arguing over whether or not there was 'F' in Niger.

The UN's World Food Programme, responsible for food aid when starvation threatens, defines famine as a 'serious food crisis made worse by governments' failure to deal with the situation'. No wonder the Niger government reacted with anger to suggestions that the designation 'F' should be applied to the situation there. President Mamadou Tandja declared it was only a 'food shortage'. The WFP was diplomatic and stuck to 'pockets of severe malnutrition'. Organizations such as Oxfam, Save the Children, Christian Aid and the British Red Cross, however, united in the British Disaster Emergency Committee, pulled no punches, mounting a fundraising campaign for 'famine in Niger'. Although caused by 'drought and locusts'.

Disagreements about the definition of famine make it hard to come up with appropriate plans of action, or to hold organizations responsible when those plans fail.

G

G7 – Group of Seven, composed of seven of the richest industrialized countries: Canada, the United Kingdom, France, Italy, Germany, Japan and the United States. Although Russia does not qualify as a major economic power, since 1998 the Russian president has attended annual meetings of the G7 – hence the term *G8 summit*.

There's also a *G77*, the largest consultative body of developing states.

Guesstimates – Where facts are lacking, as in countries that don't compile statistics, people indulge in what are known as guesstimates. Even the most respected and well-informed sources make stabs in the dark and disguise them as research results – with impunity, since no one checks the figures in countries like these. The claim that since 1991 the percentage of people in northern Uganda infected with HIV has fallen from precisely 13.8 per cent to precisely 8.7 per cent is one example of a guesstimate aimed at 'proving' that programmes to combat AIDS in Uganda have been successful. In 2003, estimates of the number of Liberians who were in acute need because of the war varied from 'hundreds of thousands' (UN) and 'one million' (AP) to 'practically the entire population of 3.2 million souls' (the American Black Caucus). The only *fact* about the condition of the Liberian people was that nobody knew what it was. AP alone gave a source, after a fashion, for its guesstimate: 'international aid organizations' that were attempting to raise funds for projects in Liberia.

G-word, the – Genocide. The United Nations Convention on the Prevention and Punishment of the Crime of Genocide defines it as 'acts committed with intent to destroy, in whole or in part, a

national, ethnic, racial or religious group'. According to the Geneva
Conventions the number of people killed is less important than the
motive for killing them. In international judicial proceedings,
genocide is regarded as 'the crime of crimes'.

According to the Charter of the United Nations, if genocide
is committed anywhere in the world, UN member states may
intervene. Since member states have no desire to do so – as we saw
with northern Iraq (1988), Rwanda (1994) and Darfur (2003 onwards)
– they play all kinds of semantic tricks to 'prove' that genocide is
not taking place, or not yet, or not really. They avoid using the
G-word.

In 2004, at the height of the 'G' in Darfur, the then UN Secretary-
General, Kofi Annan, spoke of 'a tragic humanitarian situation'.
The G7 stuck to 'massive human rights violations' and the Sudanese
government went no further than to say there was 'a problem' in
Darfur.

In 2005 the stamp of 'G' came closer for Darfur. Or so it seemed.
'The administration is currently describing the repression as ethnic
cleansing, but we see indications and elements that would start to
move you to a genocidal conclusion,' said Colin Powell, then US
Secretary of State.

In other situations the G-word is tossed around with abandon.
The Dutch animal rights lobby, for instance, described the destruction of chickens to prevent the spread of bird flu as 'genocide' and
in South Africa ministers were accused of committing genocide
when the distribution of AIDS-inhibitors took too long.

Genocide light has been used to describe ordinary mass murder, and
a country has *genocide credit* if donors give it leeway on human rights
because it has experienced genocide. See for example Rwanda.

H

Hand that feeds you mechanism – NGOs that are wholly or
partly dependent on government financing get caught up in

this mechanism. It runs counter to the Red Cross principle of independence.

Heras tactic – Warring parties often lack the time to cooperate with well-intentioned peace projects by international aid organizations. They're too busy fighting. Or they turn on the aid workers and kidnap or rob them. The resulting frustration sometimes causes the opinion to take root among aid workers that we'd do better to build a fence around conflict zones – manufactured by the world-famous fencing company Heras. 'Once the fence is in place we'll walk away and come back in a few years to see whether between them they have left anybody in one piece,' is the attitude. The Heras tactic is often proposed in the case of 'senseless' wars in darkest Africa, but former Yugoslavia, Western Sahara, Somalia and Sudan have all been candidates.

Some reject the thinking behind the Heras tactic as 'isolationism' and 'misanthropy'.

Historical suffering – 'You're expected to make money available to ease historical suffering,' former Dutch politician Paul Rosen-möller said of the interminable aid budget negotiations between the Netherlands and its former colony of Curaçao.

The conviction held by white Westerners that they bear a historical responsibility for the misdeeds of rulers of ex-colonies, even decades after independence, is sometimes referred to as *humanitarian racism*, since it fails to acknowledge the responsibilities of local populations.

Humanitarian – 1. (adj.) philanthropic; 2. (noun) a person who promotes human welfare. Not to be confused with a *human rights activist*, who defends the minimum standards to which individuals are entitled by virtue of their membership of humanity. Nor with a *humanist*, who adheres to a movement that expects mankind to be rejuvenated by, among other things, an in-depth study of Greek and Roman culture.

Humanitarians practise *humanitarianism*, defined by the International Federation of Red Cross and Red Crescent Societies as 'a desire [. . .] to prevent and alleviate human suffering wherever it may be found [. . .] and to ensure respect for the human being'. Humanitarianism gave rise to the Geneva Conventions, under which populations have a *humanitarian right* to security and welfare, even in wartime. Governments bear the primary responsibility for the security and welfare of their peoples, but rebels and insurgents too have a duty to shield civilians from military violence. *Humanitarian aid* becomes necessary when those governments, rebels and insurgents are unwilling or unable to give such protection and care. The situation is then defined as a *humanitarian crisis*. If many humanitarian organizations turn up at one place it becomes known as a *humanitarian hotspot*.

The term *humanitarian intervention* comes into play when politicians insist that the violence they are using is well intentioned, because it's designed to help people in need. NATO, for example, called its attacks on Kosovo *humanitarian bombardments*: the Serbs who were besieging Kosovo and blocking aid to the Kosovars had to be expelled. There are some who scoff that humanitarian intervention is 'philanthropic imperialism'.

Playing the humanitarian card is what you are doing, as a dictator, when you invite humanitarian aid organizations to come and run humanitarian aid projects in your country purely as a means of removing a weapon from the arsenal of those who claim you're a monster.

Complicated? Only back home. In many cultures the word 'humanitarian' doesn't exist and neither does the profession of humanitarian aid worker.

Humanitarian buzzwords – When donor governments decide that the 'aid concept *du jour*' must be tackling poverty, or reinforcing *civil society* or gender equality, then experienced aid organizations adjust their project proposals accordingly. If donors place the emphasis in their funding policy on good government, or urban development, then aid organizations do likewise. 'You just couch your memoranda, form-filling parlance, policy definitions and websites in the most up-to-the-minute jargon to please your donors,' a 'proposal writer' for an NGO confided in me.

He explained that certain buzzwords are indispensable in proposals to donors. 'Sustainable development', for instance. You can easily attach that term to anything, whether it's a project to tackle poverty, a birth-control programme or agricultural assistance. 'Birth control is the key to sustainable development' sounds just as convincing as 'tackling poverty is the key to sustainable development'.

'Globalization' is another term that can be deployed in any project proposal, as are 'women's rights' and 'democratization'. 'Democratization is the key to globalization' sounds plausible and no less topical than 'women's rights are the key to democratization'. Or the reverse: 'Democratization is the key to women's rights.' The same principle even works with 'artificial fertilizer': 'Artificial fertilizer is the key to sustainability/democratization/tackling poverty.'

Other popular themes of the day include *capacity building*, *citizen participation* and *local ownership of policies*. Hence: 'Artificial fertilizer is the key to capacity building.' And: 'Citizen participation leads to sustainable ways of tackling poverty.'

'Equal rights for women' is another subject popular with donors. So in a project proposal it's good to touch upon a *gender-balanced approach*, *gender-focused initiatives* and *gender concerns*.

Finally, since September 2001 you'd be extremely well advised to make mention of 'anti-terrorism' somewhere in your proposal. You can surely claim that thanks to your capacity building, people will no longer be driven by poverty into the arms of terrorists.

J

Jesus Brigades – Aid organizations run by fundamentalist Christians. President George W. Bush's Republican administration, which had a policy of allocating generous amounts of federal funding to Jesus Brigades, preferred to call them 'faith-based groups'.

L

Landing strip effect – If a disaster occurs beside or not far from an airstrip, as in Goma (1994), more aid organizations and media show up than when disaster strikes in, for example, Kashmir (2005), where aid organizations could reach the mountain people hit by the earthquake only by travelling on foot, by donkey or in hugely expensive chartered helicopters.

M

Marshall Plan – Legendary aid project. After the Second World War, the US donated $13 billion, plus American knowledge and expertise, to repair war-damaged Europe. It was not a strictly philanthropic act. The Marshall Plan saved Europe, but the US assured itself of a huge market that would become rich enough to buy American products.

The Marshall Plan was a success because it wasn't required to create something out of nothing like reconstruction efforts today, in Afghanistan for instance. Highly developed European culture had only to be stirred back into life. And there was just one donor. Today's reconstruction projects involve dozens of donors, stubbornly working at cross-purposes.

Millennium Development Goals – Aid project by UN member states. Between 2000 and 2015 it aims to use development aid to achieve, among other things, a rough halving of the number of poor people in the world. The most pressing questions, which have remained unanswered since the project began, are: if we're to halve the number of poor people, then what about the other half? And which half do we choose?

N

Nes-Kofi – Nickname of former UN Secretary-General Kofi Annan, who advocated further expansion of the already close cooperation between the United Nations and the business community. 'We need each other,' he said at a meeting of the International Chamber of Commerce. Helmut Maucher, chairman and CEO of Nestlé, was jubilant, saying to members, 'We've achieved what we wanted! We now find ourselves at the centre of the debate.' The business community doesn't 'just' want to be a player in the future of the world, it wants to *be* the future.

The financial neglect of the UN by its own member states over many years is driving the organization further and further into the arms of business. The Bill and Melinda Gates Foundation donates tens of millions to UN projects to combat AIDS, and in a Coca-Cola Company project, Coca-Cola trucks drive around Africa handing out condoms instead of fizzy drinks. No doubt to the disappointment of Africans. UN member states look on with satisfaction: 'Things Go Better With Coke!'

Never again – From events in Darfur, northern Iraq, Rwanda and Bosnia, we can deduce that 'never again' should be interpreted to mean not 'never again genocide' but 'never again an attempt to exterminate the Jewish people by German Nazis'.

NGOism – When aid is a country's most important economic activity. The term was invented in Afghanistan, where 2,355 NGOs were registered, 333 of them international (2004), as against virtually no ordinary businesses or investors.

O

ODA – Official Development Assistance. The almost $120 billion per year that the thirty rich industrialized countries of the OECD set aside for development assistance. ODA comes in many guises. It most commonly takes the form of bilateral aid (from one government to another). In 2008 this rose by 12.5 per cent compared to 2007. In recent years bilateral aid has come under fire, with critics accusing it of being ineffective and of fostering corruption in recipient countries. In second place comes multilateral aid (from several governments to one government), followed by institutional aid from governments to institutions such as the UN, the World Bank, the IMF and the EU.

The OECD expects that, despite a deepening of the current worldwide recession, flows of aid will increase further. An inventory of government intentions through into 2010 shows that total aid contributions will rise by 11 per cent.

Omnipotence, our own – 'Western fantasy. [. . .] Give some money and all will be well, as if the problems of Africa are just the results of our not paying enough attention.'[9]

One dollar a day – The poverty line as defined by the World Bank. Seen by many economists outside the World Bank as arbitrary and meaningless, since a dollar is worth almost nothing in some countries while it goes quite a long way in others.

Own fault effect – Also known as the *yet-another-stupid-African-war effect*. A term used when donors make less money available for a humanitarian disaster with an obviously political cause, such as a war, than aid organizations had hoped. Victims of natural disasters, such as drought or a tsunami, can often count on more sympathy.

A related phenomenon is the *seen-it-before syndrome,* which encourages thrift among donors if a disaster is no more dramatic and deadly than an earlier one. Fundraisers try to combat this syndrome by portraying an event as, for example, 'the worst humanitarian crisis ever' or 'the greatest threat to humanity in modern history'.

P

Perverse incentive – A phenomenon in which a recipient of aid resources, whether the government of a poor country, an aid organization or an individual, knows better than to wind up an aid project on the grounds of success. Being needy pays.

Phantom aid – On average, 60 per cent of official aid from donor governments is phantom aid. *Tied aid* falls under this heading – the money never leaves the donor country but is paid straight into the bank accounts of a range of development-aid innovation platforms, consciousness-raising and base-broadening initiatives, interest groups and lobby groups, policy advisers and Third World experts. Other forms of tied aid oblige NGOs to source all products and services in the donor country, even those that could be acquired far more cheaply in the crisis zone itself. Many major donor governments are therefore principally subsidizing their own economies. They have no scruples about paying the resulting transport costs (for people and supplies) and import duties out of their aid budgets.

The US is the largest donor of phantom aid: 70–80 per cent of all American government aid money is paid to American organizations: American factories, American contractors and American transport companies. It has been estimated that the cost of reconstruction in Iraq, America's largest aid project, could have been reduced by up to 90 per cent had the rebuilding of roads, bridges, factories, power plants and water-supply infrastructure been contracted to Iraqi rather than American companies. More than half of all American aid to Iraq is spent on accommodating, provisioning and protecting the thousands of Americans who travel to Iraq to get the job done (see also **Playing the chaos**).

Canada, Germany, Japan and France come next on the list of contributors of phantom aid. They insist that up to 60 per cent of their aid budgets must be used to buy products and services from within their own countries, ranging from steamrollers for laying roads and advisers for ministries in project countries all the way down to cooking pots for refugee families and drugs to treat AIDS. Researchers from the anti-corruption organization Tiri have calculated that as a result reconstruction operations in Lebanon, East Timor, Afghanistan, Bosnia and Eritrea were hugely more expensive than they need have been.

Ninety per cent of bilateral aid given by Great Britain, Norway, Denmark and the Netherlands is not tied, but then again, the sums these countries donate through the EU are to a great degree tied.

Phantom aid includes *old money*, already pledged to poor countries but later assigned to other purposes and then pledged a second time. Much of the funding for tsunami victims in Sri Lanka and Aceh, for example, was deducted from promised aid programmes to combat hunger and disease in Africa.

Playing the chaos – An activity indulged in by contractors implementing reconstruction projects in war zones, with hundreds of millions of dollars each year in non-itemized invoices as the jackpot. Contractors have become the most financially successful arm of the aid industry, along with consultancy businesses (see **TAs**).

Paid out of budgets intended as aid to local populations, contractors (usually based in the West) are hired by donors and NGOs to build or repair roads, bridges, airports, factories, schools, clinics, power stations and water-treatment plants. Even in a stable and orderly country like the Netherlands, building contractors represent the business sector most susceptible to fraud; in the chaos and lawlessness of warring or war-ravaged countries, where opportunities for supervision are limited or entirely lacking, this occupational group invariably goes wild. 'Just plaster over any shoddy work' is their watch phrase. Investigations into contractors working in Liberia, Bosnia-Herzegovina, Lebanon and Afghanistan and reports from Somalia, Congo and Sudan reveal that billions of dollars entrusted to them have 'evaporated'. The reconstruction of Iraq promises to become the greatest evaporation scandal in the history of aid provision. By mid-2008, $117 billion had been spent ($50 billion of it from the American treasury) and more than 600 firms were working in Iraq under contract to the American government, managing to create a mighty shambles of faked invoices and untraceable bookkeeping.

Some examples: in hundreds of cases it was impossible to find out how aid contracts had come into being. One contractor issued an invoice for $9.5 billion based on receipts that added up to less than $2 billion. Many jobs were paid for in cash taken from a safe in the basement of one of Saddam Hussein's former palaces. Sums of $2 million were counted out in $100 bills in exchange for handwritten receipts. Shadow companies were set up in the Cayman Islands purely to write fake invoices. Tax evasion, missed deadlines, services charged for but never rendered, deliveries of faulty equipment, circumvention of controls, rapid staff turnover such that checks were begun but rarely completed, staff shortages, contracts that went to the quickest rather than the best, and executives who made changes to contracts worth many millions of dollars with a quick scrawl or a verbal commitment.

The Halliburton firm of contractors, which is suspected of fraud worth billions of dollars during the reconstruction of Iraq, popped up in New Orleans after Hurricane Katrina. Twelve billion dollars was promptly unaccounted for. It gained New Orleans the nickname 'Baghdad under Water'.

Contractors also take on jobs traditionally performed by soldiers, from driving army trucks to staffing the laundries that wash the troops' clothing, and interrogating prisoners. Aid budgets enable them to earn up to $1,000 a day. With an estimated 180,000 employees, contracting firms in Iraq now have more people on the ground than the US army (160,000). Some estimates suggest they also supply more staff to UN peace missions than the UN member states themselves.

Programme area – The term for a disaster zone after international aid organizations have landed.

Project proposal – 'Well spoken is well funded': the money goes not to the best idea but to the best-written project proposal, as everybody knows. Which is why aid agencies employ professional 'proposal writers'.

Those who have mastered the art can make nothing at all look extremely impressive. A project at Port Loko, Sierra Leone, financed by the British government's Department for International Development (DFID), was presented as follows: 'supports resettlement and reintegration of ex-combatants and displaced persons [. . .] to increase economic activities in Port Loko district'. It was all about 'establishing resettled and reintegrated communities contributing in the long term to the establishment of sustainable peace and security. The expected output of the pilot programme is to improve the standard of living in terms of economic and public infrastructure, including rural road networks and markets and increased food security.'

When the programme was up and running, I met its coordinator at the roadside next to his project, dressed in a purple batik shirt, bare white legs below khaki shorts. At his feet were twenty-five former child soldiers, or teenagers who claimed that's what they were, digging a deep hole with second-hand spades.

'After lunch I'll get them to fill the hole in again and tomorrow we'll dig a new one further along and the day after that another,' the project leader said with satisfaction. He paid 'his' boys 50 euro cents a day, thereby fulfilling all the promises of the original project proposal. I guess.

R

Race against the clock – Despite vastly expensive early-warning systems installed all over the globe, satellite coverage and the semi-permanent presence of foreign aid organizations in poor countries, aid provision always seems to degenerate into a 'race against the clock'. At least so it seems from press releases issued by humanitarian organizations.

Recycling – A concept familiar to every refugee-camp resident in the world, although he may call it something else. In essence it means that a refugee will surreptitiously leave a camp and then report at the gate again under a different name. That way he gets to keep his first ration card and is given a second one with his new name on it. The recycler can then eat twice as much as before or, if he sells his second serving, buy things he needs but won't get from the UNHCR. The proceeds from second cards are the basis of large shadow economies in camps. Thousands of refugees protect themselves against malnutrition this way.

Refugee – A person who 'owing to a well-founded fear of being persecuted for reasons of race, religion, nationality, membership of a particular social group, or political opinion, is outside the country of his nationality, and is unable to or, owing to such fear, is unwilling to avail himself of the protection of that country'.

There are tens of millions of refugees in the world and in most cases it's impossible to check whether they fit this UNHCR definition. As a result almost everyone who reports to the gates of a UNHCR refugee camp has an automatic right to relief.

Refugee status is coveted, since according to international legal provisions, refugees cannot be returned to the dangers from which they've escaped. Major contaminants of worldwide refugee statistics are *economic refugees*, who are fleeing poverty. International rules state that they are not 'genuine' refugees. Other elements that muddy the statistical waters are 'refugee warriors', combatants disguised as refugees, who come to UNHCR camps to rest up and share a few meals before heading out for the front line again (see also **Safe enclaves**).

IDPs are 'Internally Displaced Persons', who have been uprooted but are still within their own countries. They do not fall under the remit of the UNHCR (which almost exclusively 'handles' refugees who are outside their home countries); instead they are the responsibility of their own governments. For many IDPs this is reason enough to continue walking until they cross the border and become refugees.

Relief hardware – Lorries and fuel for aid projects in the Horn of Africa, equipment for clinics in Tanzania, medicines for projects in Mongolia, shuttle helicopters and field kitchens for UN peace-keepers in Liberia and Haiti, telecoms facilities, generators and tents for refugee-reception projects in Chad, aluminium window frames and doors for project offices in the Great Lakes Region, refugee-camp inventories for Afghanistan, corrugated iron and cement for reintegration projects in Burundi, computers and office equipment for Iraq, white Land Cruisers, radios, tarpaulins, jerrycans, pots and pans for Darfur, etc.

Resilience – The strength and calm that enable a person or a community to recover from a disaster so that they emerge from it even stronger than before. A quality that is always greeted with some surprise when detected in people in poor countries, whom we habitually associate with helplessness.

Sometimes the discovery of resilience in poor people may even bring with it a slight sense of disappointment. 'But don't you realize you'll get a new house from *us*?' an aid worker with Médecins sans Frontières, mildly indignant, asked an industriously carpenting man in Aceh after the tsunami.

S

Safe enclaves – Traditional concept in the laws of war. Territories where civilians caught up in a conflict can find safety and wait for the fighting to end. Enclaves seem safe because of the presence of international peacekeeping forces and/or aid organizations, but their protected status is not laid down in any statute book and in practice it often turns out to be illusory. Attacks frequently follow, since 'safety zones' are hardly ever strictly civilian as they should be according to the laws of war. Soldiers and militias almost always mingle with refugees to get a share of food aid deliveries and use the medical facilities on offer.

Among the better known 'safe' areas are the Zône Turquoise for Hutus in south-western Rwanda, which was 'guarded' by UN blue helmets until shot to pieces by Rwandan government troops in 1995, and Srebrenica for Bosnian Muslims, supposedly protected by the peacekeeping force UNPROFOR but cleared amid much bloodshed by Bosnian Serbs that same year.

Salvation Army – 'Everywhere you go in Africa, you'd think you were in a Salvation Army junk store. We grow excellent cotton in Africa, but the West doesn't want to buy it. They'd rather subsidize their own cotton farmers and bring us their own worn-out rags,' a Senegalese agricultural economist said about clothing-collection campaigns for poor countries in rich countries.

Smile and wave strategy – A military tactic that armies use as they move around in humanitarian territories, in order to conquer not only countries but the *hearts and minds* of local populations. The thinking behind it is that people are significantly less likely to attack you if you're providing them with food and other support. The strategy forms part of what's known as *coherent humanitarian action*, in which military, political and humanitarian initiatives are different aspects of a shared enterprise. Soldiers need to be able to switch from aggression to tenderness on command.

Coherent humanitarian military action is sometimes referred to as *blue helmetlike*.

Spoils of peace – The millions in aid that pour into a country or region when a war ends. Promises of a 'peace dividend' are often an element of peace negotiations, intended to tempt warring parties to sign a treaty.

States, recipient – *Quasi states* are those that have been able to survive since independence only with the help of foreign aid. 'Negative sovereignty' is another name for such total dependence. In a *predator state* the government feeds itself on resources it steals from its own subjects. In a *shadow state* the state is a façade behind which leaders survive by decidedly unstatesmanlike means, such as the smuggling of drugs and raw materials. In a *failing state* policy is still formulated by the government but no longer implemented. Government workers are a symbolic presence; their work has a ritual character. The army and police take priority in the allocation of scarce national incomes and some kind of economic policy is in place but only because foreign donors demand it. Finally, the *failed state* is a country so unstable that it has ceased to exist. Somalia is one.

Cynics claim that the entire heart of Africa is in fact a *stateless void*, containing nothing but mess and misery.

T

TAs – Technical assistants, consultants. After contractors, TAs are the main recipients of developmental and reconstruction budgets (see **Playing the chaos**). The sums aid organizations can spend in poor countries and crisis zones are dwarfed by the turnovers of TA companies.

TAs are hired by donors, by financial institutions such as the World Bank and by development banks, embassies, the United Nations and large NGOs. In Africa alone an estimated 100,000 TAs provide expertise on every subject imaginable, from democratization, agriculture and economics to polio prevention, tax law, women's rights, ground-water levels, potato diseases and cotton markets. Donors also like to place them in strategic positions in ministries in recipient countries to check that their aid contributions are being properly spent.

In the reconstruction project that is Afghanistan, the number of TAs has been estimated at 3,000 plus. 'There are more consultants in Kabul than fleas and dogs,' sighed an employee at the US embassy there.

At least 25 per cent of total ODA (see under O) is paid to TAs. In fact mega-donor America pays them almost half its total aid budget.

TAs are sometimes referred to as *Thousand Dollar Men*, after their average daily allowance. Then there are the costs of their security, accommodation, transport, dinners, etc.

One TA said: 'When I applied, I had a fantasy of myself as a kind of dashing secret agent on a mission to exotic countries, lazing next to hotel swimming pools with a martini in my hand, surrounded by beautiful women in bikinis. And it turned out that's just what it was like!'

Former Afghan finance minister Ashraf Ghani reckoned only 10 per cent of the one hundred TAs in total that various donors had attached to his ministry were 'first class'. Thirty-five per cent were 'tolerable', he said, and the rest were 'absolutely awful'.

Teresa, Mother – '*Pecunia non olet*': money doesn't stink. Not even to Mother Teresa, who was beatified in 2003. She stubbornly refused to give the Indian government access to her accounts, as Indian law requires foreign missionaries to do. In his book *The Missionary Position – Mother Teresa in Theory and Practice* (1995), journalist Christopher Hitchens revealed that the little mother had parked some of the millions donated to her in foreign bank accounts. In one account in New York City alone she had $50 million. But when she died in 1997 her clinic was just as basic and medically backward as before she became rich and famous. The little mother herself preferred to go to modern hospitals in California when anything was wrong with her.

Third World – Term that emerged in the 1950s to refer to countries belonging neither to NATO (the First World) nor to the Eastern Bloc (Second World). Later a synonym for 'poor countries'.

Tsunami – An autonomous concept, but applicable in any desired combination: *tsunami country*, *tsunami summit*, *tsunami orphan*, *tsunami volunteer*, *tsunami money*, etc. The tsunami in Asia on Boxing Day 2004 released *a philanthropic tsunami*, or a *tsunami of generosity*. Aid 'inundated' the affected areas *like a second tsunami* and *with the speed of a tsunami*.

Other disaster zones were somewhat jealous of this *tsunami of attention*. 'Sierra Leone's civil war was a tsunami that lasted ten years, but without the headlines,' aid organizations working in Sierra Leone at the time complained. UN Undersecretary-General for Humanitarian Affairs Jan Egeland pleaded for more money for Darfur, arguing that the 'tsunami' there might eventually claim more victims than the one in the Indian Ocean. Since the tsunami, 'forgotten crises' like these have in fact been labelled *silent tsunamis*, in the hope that donors will sit up a little in response to that description.

According to a number of aid organizations with creative communication skills, the highlands of Pakistan experienced a *mountain tsunami* with the earthquake of 2005. The overwhelming flood of commemorations to mark the first anniversary of the tsunami was called the *tsunami tsunami*.

U

UNHCR – Time to take out the calculator. African governments create the biggest and costliest streams of refugees on earth. Yet African countries contribute next to nothing to the annual budget of over $2 billion available to the UN refugee organization UNHCR, which is charged with taking care of the world's refugees. In 2008 the African Union donated $600,000 to the UNHCR. Morocco then threw another $500,000 into the UNHCR pot bilaterally and South Africa $145,000. This means that between them the African countries contributed just a fraction more money to the African refugee problem than the impoverished Czech Republic did on its own. The budget for worldwide refugee relief is derived almost entirely from mega-donors such as the US ($510,000 million in 2008), the EC ($130 million), Japan ($110 million), Sweden ($105 million) and the Netherlands ($85,000 million). The UK donated $57,000 million in 2008, putting it in seventh place (after Norway who donated $61,000 million).

United Nations – 'The UN wasn't created to lead humanity to heaven but to save it from hell.'[10]

W

Warehousing – The 'penning up' of refugees in camps. Countries bordering on war zones prefer to keep refugees in one place, in a camp, in the hope that one day they'll go home. Letting refugees wander about freely means risking they'll settle in your country and build a new life. Of the 10.5 million refugees worldwide, 7.5 million spend more than ten years penned up.[11] Some refugee peoples are warehoused for the rest of their lives, even for generations.

Warehousing is not without dangers. Refugee camps, often over-crowded, are hotbeds of infectious disease. Cholera and dysentery rarely fail to strike, but the description sometimes heard in aid worker circles of camps as 'condomless environments' provides food for thought as well.

Moreover, warehoused refugees are at the mercy of sometimes malicious camp leaders, marauding gangs of bandits and the philanthropy of Western donors. When the war from which camp-dwellers have fled no longer interests the donors, aid budgets for the camps will decline to just below the level needed to completely dispel hunger and disease.

At the same time, well-financed camps where life is better than it is outside are another unintended outcome. 'Rich' camps become known as 'tourist camps', since donor delegations and diplomats are sent there to be taken on guided tours of successful aid projects.

Local residents, often desperately poor themselves, may grow jealous of the prosperity in rich camps and slip in for a share of the aid rations, health care and, above all, schooling for their children.

Being warehoused, hanging about in a camp without anything to do, can generate frustration and resentment. Afghanistan's Taliban movement, for example, was born in Afghan refugee camps in Pakistan.

Weapons of mass salvation – Vaccinations.

White elephants – Large, costly infrastructural development aid projects that are not economically viable. 'We like building roads,' a representative of the European Commission in West Africa told me in 2006. 'That's quick and easy. You hire contractors, order up a shipment of asphalt and slice a road through the bush. Looks good, especially if you paint some nice white lines on it, and you can write in your report that you've laid so many kilometres of highway. The fact that the country has nothing to drive on a road like that and therefore little use for it isn't our problem.'

Next on the list of popular white elephant projects come schools and clinics. 'We write in our report that this year we've built, say, thirty-five of the things, but that doesn't mean any more than that we've had some bricklaying done in thirty-five places. We don't provide doctors and teachers to go in them,' said the EC man. 'The countries themselves have to take care of that.' Or not. Just as long as the donors are happy. And donors like aid that's measurable and quantifiable. 'The results are all that count,' said American USAID to NGOs that were asking for finance. 'If you cannot measure results, if you cannot show what you've done, other partners will be found,' former director Andrew Natsios explained.

White elephants aren't confined to Africa. The majority of Iraqis are still without electric lighting, since there's no money to keep the power stations reconstructed by the Americans running. 'Americans are investing hundreds of millions in Iraq. The capacity is not there to maintain it,' Mark Oviatt, who oversees American reconstruction work in Iraq, told the *New York Times*.

Poor countries are full of the resulting empty buildings and unused roads. Donor statistics are too, but under the heading of 'completed projects'.

White Land Cruiser crowd – Aid workers who move through the world's disaster zones in large white four-wheel-drives with aerials whipping on the roofs, on their way to development aid projects or to the local bars. In Afghanistan, where at one point there were over 3,000 national and international aid and donor organizations, they are known as the *Toyota Taliban*. In Sudan they're called the *white ooze*.

World Bank – The largest development aid institution of all, with a budget running to many tens of billions of euros a year. The world's richest countries are members and they fill the kitty. Created in 1945 out of the ashes of the Great Depression, Nazism, the Second World War and the United Nations Monetary Conference at Bretton Woods in America, the World Bank was set up to provide loans for the reconstruction of Europe. Later, non-European crisis states became eligible to ask it for help.

The conditions that any country wanting a loan from the World Bank has to fulfil are drastic in their effects. The bitterest pills are always the *structural adjustment programmes.* 'One size fits all': government expenditure must be cut, subsidies abolished and masses of government workers fired. Leaders of poor countries who use public money for personal shopping trips and stuff their ministries with their own followers are usually little inclined to cooperate with structural adjustments. If they do eventually sign up, it's referred to as 'swallowing the medicine'.

Western anti-imperialists are generally against the World Bank. Because the US dominates the bank, they regard the terms and conditions as enforced acceptance of American ideology, economic and otherwise.

Whether such acceptance produces the desired results, no one knows. What exactly became of the half-trillion dollars the World Bank has paid out to poor countries since it was founded in 1946 is largely unclear. Investigations by the bank itself in 2005 showed that in the preceding five years the results of only 2 per cent of the bank's own projects had been evaluated.

Wristbands – At demonstrations and protest marches you can tell what people are campaigning about from the colour of the wristbands they're wearing. 'Look Good While You Do Good' seems to be the motto of the wristband crowd. Orange wristbands are for respect, red against violence, green against genocide in Darfur, white against poverty, black-and-white against racism.

Racing cyclist Lance Armstrong instigated the wristband rage. In 2004 he launched a yellow wristband against cancer and sold more than 20 million worldwide. Even prime ministers and members of royal families have been spotted wearing wristbands.

Sometimes a battle for a colour breaks out, as it did when the Tilburg branch of COC (Centre for Culture and Leisure, the euphemistic name of the oldest lesbian, gay, bisexual and transgender organization in the world) launched a pink wristband for its campaign against increasing intolerance of homosexuals, even though pink had already been claimed by supporters of Kylie Minogue's breast cancer campaign.

For victims of the tsunami, a band of black neoprene, the material used to make diving suits, came on to the market.

For all that, wristband campaigns are surely better than 'Panties for Peace' or Timberland boots with 'Stomp Out Genocide' soles.

Acknowledgements

Between this book's conception and its birth in 2008, five years went by. I'm grateful to everyone who was there during its gestation, whether briefly or for a long time, intensively, or just out of companionship. There are a number of people I would like to thank in particular.

Tjitske Lingsma and Minka Nijhuis, friends, journalists and editors of this book. Phenomenal in all three manifestations.

Maartje Wildeman, my agent. She e-mailed: 'I'm curious to know what you'll make of me in those acknowledgements of yours. A rowdy lout? Every publisher's nightmare? Just don't lay it on too thick!' I wouldn't dare. Maartje, you were a bridge over sometimes deep, black waters. Thank you.

Bart Vos, writer, mountaineer and instantly prepared to help edit the book. Your comments were extremely welcome and always on target.

Patricia Hofmeester, friend, photographer and reader of the manuscript. Always there, even when I was in a real bind.

Jos Moerkamp, friend and colleague. He too read the manuscript and fine-tuned it unerringly.

Arita Baaijens, friend and writer, whose suggestions made the book better.

Lieve Joris and Marek Stawski, friends, always clearly in view on my sidelines, cheering and full of good advice.

Bart Kuiter, comrade, who gave my years in Sierra Leone a silver lining with his humour and his generosity in sharing his knowledge.

Max Chevalier, committed to 'his' children in Murray Town Camp in Freetown, who for that reason helped me to disentangle their fate.

My home front, the pillars of my existence: Mam, Noor, Thiba and Neal.

Dick Voorsluijs, my brother-in-law, and Gerard Hemrika, a friend of many years. Without them too, this book would not exist.

Rozenberg Publishers: Auke, Sunny, Silvia and Ingrid, who assisted me however and whenever they could.

Jan Michael, literary agent, thanks for all your efforts in furthering my books' international careers.

Thanks to Plien van Albada and Uitgeverij Balans for your confidence.

Liz Waters, translator, thanks for your patience.

This book has been financed in part by subsidies from the Fund for Extraordinary Journalistic Projects (www.fondsbjp.nl) and the Democracy and Media Foundation (www.stdem.org), both based in Amsterdam.

The five years spent producing this book were not without drama. I'm thinking especially of Rob Bland. He translated my previous book, *We Did Nothing*. Rob refused to rest until the book had been taken up by foreign publishers and carried further. Even that wasn't enough for him. On his deathbed he put the book in an envelope with the intention of getting it into the hands of Colin Powell. 'My final attempt to make the bastard see the light,' he said.

We were planning to work on this new book together, but Rob died of cancer in October 2004. I have a great deal to thank him for. Rob, in case you can hear me: this one's for you!

Note

My argument has far more to do with processes and phenomena than with individuals. I have changed one or two names in the interests of that larger truth.

Notes

Preface: Imagine. You get a phone call . . .

1 Henri Dunant, *A Memory of Solferino*, ICRC, 1863.
2 Hugh Small, *Florence Nightingale: Avenging Angel*, St Martin's Press, New York, 1998, reprinted 2000.
3 G. Frerks, B. Klem, S. van Laar and M. van Klingeren, *Principles and Pragmatism: Civil–Military Action in Afghanistan and Liberia*, University of Utrecht and Cordaid, May 2006.

1. Goma: a 'total ethical disaster'

1 Fiona Terry, *Condemned to Repeat?: The Paradox of Humanitarian Action*, Cornell University Press, Ithaca, 2002.
2 The closest harbours for supplies of food and medicines were more than 1,000 kilometres away, on the coast of Tanzania. There were no direct rail connections with the camps, and mountains, rain and a lack of roads in the Great Lakes Region made the operation even more expensive. (See *The International Response to Conflict and Genocide: Lessons from the Rwanda Experience*, Steering Committee of the Joint Evaluation of Emergency Assistance, May 1996.)
3 Terry, *Condemned to Repeat?*
4 Ibid.
5 *New Yorker*, 4 August 1997.

2. Contract fever

1 Alexander Cooley and James Ron, 'The NGO Scramble: Organizational Insecurity and the Political Economy of Transnational Action', *International Security*, Vol. 27 (2002), no. 1 (Summer), pp. 5–39.

2   Fiona Terry, *Condemned to Repeat?: The Paradox of Humanitarian Action*, Cornell University Press, Ithaca, 2002.

3   Cooley and Ron, 'The NGO Scramble'.

4   *'Pourquoi nous quittons les camps de réfugiés rwandais'*, newsletter to individual donors to MSF France, December 1994.

5   Terry, *Condemned to Repeat?*

6   *Newsweek International*, 5 September 2005.

7   The OECD keeps a record of the sums its thirty member states make available annually for Official Development Assistance (ODA). By far the most generous ODA donor, at around $26 billion a year (2008), is the United States. 'No one else even comes close to us,' beamed Andrew Natsios, former director of USAID, which administers the American aid budget. In second place comes Germany with almost $14 billion. Next comes Great Britain (more than $11 billion), followed by France (just under $11 billion), Japan ($9 billion) and the Netherlands (just under $7 billion). ODA comes from a number of non-OECD members too, such as the EC (European Commission) at more than $13 billion (2008), South Korea and Turkey (over $0.5 billion each), Poland (over $386 million) and the Czech Republic (over $100 million). Total ODA in 2008 was almost $120 billion.

 Relatively new players in the aid market, such as China and India, Islamic and African charities, and large philanthropic organizations such as the Bill and Melinda Gates Foundation, pump several more billions of dollars a year into aid, outside the ODA system. Then there are the church plates, collecting tins, funds, associations, bingo nights, etc. in many countries, which add further billions of dollars. The magazine *Foreign Affairs* estimates that American public and private 'development aid' amounts to $35 billion a year. The largest recipients of ODA are Iraq, Nigeria, Indonesia, Afghanistan, China and Sudan. Official humanitarian aid, or first-aid for humanitarian crises resulting from war and natural disasters, totals over $11.2 billion in 2008. The US remained the biggest single donor of humanitarian aid, accounting for 38 per cent ($4.3 billion) of the total in 2008. The next biggest donors in 2008 were the European Commission ($1.9 billion) and the United Kingdom ($1.1 billion).

8 Pieter Broertjes, editor-in-chief of the Dutch newspaper *de Volkskrant*, in a debate about 'new and old media' held in De Balie, a centre for culture and public debate in Amsterdam, 21 May 2008.

9 Quoted by Reuters, May 1998.

10 Marc Broere, *Berichten over armoede: een journalistieke kijk op ontwikkelingssamenwerking*, KIT Publishers, Amsterdam, 2009.

11 Dutch daily newspaper *Trouw*, 2 May 1995.

12 *Daily Telegraph*, 10 June 2004.

13 Dutch Radio 1, 16 May 2008.

14 *CNN News*, 25 August 2003.

15 *Los Angeles Times*, 6 July 2007.

16 *Trouw*, 26 February 1997.

17 Ibid.

18 Nick Davies, *Flat Earth News*, Chatto & Windus, 2008.

3. *MONGOs*

1 *New York Times*, 10 July 2004.

2 Agence France Presse, 20 February 2005.

3 Dutch daily newspaper *Metro*, 1 February 2006.

4 Bill Clinton, *Giving: How Each of Us Can Change the World*, Alfred A. Knopf, New York, 2007.

5 Overseas Development Institute, *The International Response to Conflict and Genocide: Lessons from the Rwanda Experience*, London, May 1996.

6 Lau Schulpen, *Development in the 'Africa for Beginners'; Dutch Private Initiatives in Ghana and Malawi*, CIDIN, Nijmegen, 2007.

7 VPRO television's history programme *Andere Tijden* (Other Times), 28 January 2003.

8 *Kansas City Star*, 5 June 2001 onwards.

4. *Donor darlings*

1 *Washington Post*, 24 December 2000.

5. Aid as a weapon of war

1 *New York Times*, 10 July 2004.

2 Fabrice Weissman, *L'aide humanitaire dans la dynamique du conflit libérien*, Fondation Médecins sans Frontières, Paris, May 1996.

3 Dutch weekly *Vrij Nederland*, 9 December 2006.

4 Roy Gutman, David Rieff and Anthony Dworkin (eds.), *Crimes of War 2.0: What the Public Should Know*, Norton & Company, New York and London, 2007.

5 Fiona Terry, *Condemned to Repeat?: The Paradox of Humanitarian Action*, Cornell University Press, Ithaca, 2002.

6 *New York Times*, 9 July 2004.

7 Max Glaser, *Negotiated Access: Humanitarian Engagement with Armed Non-State Actors*, Carr Center for Human Rights Policy, Harvard University, May 2004.

8 Clea Kahn and Elena Lucchi (Humanitarian Affairs Advisors for MSF Operational Centre Amsterdam), *Humanitarian Exchange Magazine*, Humanitarian Practice Network at ODI, Issue 43, June 2009.

6. Refugee warriors

1 Dave Eggers, *What Is the What*, McSweeney's, San Francisco, 2006.

2 Ibid.

3 Samantha Power, *Chasing the Flame: Sergio Vieira de Mello and the Fight to Save the World*, The Penguin Press, New York, 2008.

7. The hunger weapon

1 Quoted in Alex de Waal, *Famine Crimes: Politics and the Disaster Relief Industry in Africa*, African Rights and The International African Institute, 1997.

2 Nathaniel H. Goetz, *Humanitarian Issues in the Biafra Conflict*, Pepperdine University School of Public Policy, California, 2001.

3 T. Allen and D. Styan, 'A Right to Interfere? Bernard Kouchner and the New Humanitarianism', *Journal of International Development*, 12, no. 6 (2000).

4 Amartya Sen, *Foreign Policy*, May/June 2009.

5 WFP director James Morris in consultation with the UN Security Council, 30 June 2005.

6 Marita Vihervuori in *Crimes of War 2.0: What the Public Should Know*, Norton & Company, New York and London, 2007.

7 David Rieff in *Crimes of War 2.0: What the Public Should Know*, Norton & Company, New York and London, 2007.

8. When recipients call the shots

1 David Rieff, 'Cruel to be Kind', *Guardian*, 25 June 2005.

2 Dutch magazine *onzeWereld*, May 1995.

3 Naomi Klein in the *Guardian*, 23 June 2003.

4 Millard Burr, *Quantifying Genocide in Southern Sudan and the Nuba Mountains 1983–1998*, US Committee for Refugees, 1998.

5 *Independent*, 17 October 2007.

9. Afghaniscam

1 *New York Times*, 30 March 2004.

2 The full text of this part of the speech by President George W. Bush to the US Congress after 9/11 runs:

We will direct every resource at our command – every means of diplomacy, every tool of intelligence, every instrument of law enforcement, every financial influence, and every necessary weapon of war – to the disruption and to the defeat of the global terror network. We are a country awakened to danger and called to defend freedom. Our grief has turned to anger, and anger to resolution. Whether we bring our enemies to justice, or bring justice to our enemies, justice will be done. Every nation, in every region, now has a decision to make. Either you are with us, or you are with the terrorists. From this day forward, any nation that continues to harbor or support terrorism will be regarded by the United States as a hostile regime.

3 Colin Powell in a speech to the National Foreign Policy Conference for Leaders of Non-Governmental Organizations, 26 October 2001.
4 *New York Times*, 4 August 2004.
5 OECD report, 'A Development Co-operation Lens on Terrorism Prevention', 2003.
6 Médecins sans Frontières France website, 16 September 2004.
7 In October 2008 a report by the British National Audit Office (NAO) revealed that millions of pounds of official British aid for the reconstruction of Afghanistan had been wasted as a result of mismanagement and corruption. The NAO found that the Department for International Development (DFID) was failing to 'achieve all or most of its objectives'. Some of the problems, the report said, were due to a lack of checks made on local partners in projects because site visits were too dangerous (*Independent*, 16 October 2008).

In May 2009 DFID produced its own internal assessment. What the NAO had said was true: millions of pounds had been wasted. By 2007 DFID was running fifty-eight projects in Afghanistan with a value of about £520 million, including £317 million from the fund run by the World Bank. In 2006–7, more than half DFID's large projects were deemed likely to fail, excluding those it financed through the World Bank's fund. Only a quarter of DFID projects were rated successful in 2006, with 4.5 per cent rated 'value for money'.

Among the examples singled out in the report was a programme in Helmand. DFID had paid for 300 wells to be dug in an area prone to drought without first carrying out a geological survey. Some of the wells had since run dry as the water table retreated. The report found that DFID's risk assessment had ignored lawlessness and corruption in the region. Other reasons why projects failed or ended 'with little evidence of tangible benefit' were 'poor planning', 'a lack of transparency' and 'failed delivery' (*The Times*, 22 May 2009).

8 'The Failed State We're In', *Prospect Magazine*, June 2008.

9 Agence France Presse, 30 January 2006.

10 *Washington Post*, 2 September 2009.

11 IPS, 24 January 2009.

12 *De Volkskrant*, 29 May 2008.

13 Joseph Stiglitz with Linda J. Bilmes, *The Three Trillion Dollar War: The True Cost of the Iraq Conflict*, W. W. Norton, New York, March 2008.

10. The logic of the humanitarian era

1 James Morris in a statement before the UN Security Council, 27 June 2005.

2 Kofi Annan at the presentation of the UN Consolidated Appeal 2004 for aid to poor countries.

3 *Columbia Journalism Review*, July 2005.

4 Lieutenant-General Roméo Dallaire, *Shake Hands with the Devil: The Failure of Humanity in Rwanda*, Random House, Canada, 2003.

5 Ibid.

6 Thabo Mbeki, 'Building a Better Africa', *Washington Post*, 10 June 2004.

7 James Morris in a statement before the UN Security Council, 27 June 2005.

8 *Independent*, 18 March 2004.

9 Afrol News, 4 May 2004.

10 *Witness to Truth*, Report of the Sierra Leone Truth and Reconciliation Commission, 5 October 2004.

Afterword: Ask them questions

1 P. T. Bauer, *Equality, the Third World, and Economic Delusion*, Harvard University Press, Cambridge, Mass., 1981.

2 The Sphere Project, *Humanitarian Charter and Minimum Standards in Disaster Response*, Oxfam Publishing, Oxford, 2004.

3 Clea Kahn and Elena Lucchi (Humanitarian Affairs Advisors for MSF Operational Centre Amsterdam), *Humanitarian Exchange Magazine*, Humanitarian Practice Network at ODI, Issue 43, June 2009.

Aid Speak

1 See also Binyavanga Wainaina in *Granta 92* (Winter 2005).

2 Minka Nijhuis, *Het Huis van Khala*, Amsterdam, Balans, 2008.

3 Report of the ECHO–ICRC conference 'Humanitarian Action – Perception and Security', 28 March 1998.

4 Amartya Sen, *Development as Freedom*, Oxford Paperbacks, 2001.

5 Bram Posthumus, *Vice Versa*, March 2004.

6 IMF Working Paper 'Aid and the Dutch Disease in Low-Income Countries', prepared by Mwanza Nkusu, March 2004.

7 Interview, Overseas Development Institute, 9 October 2002.

8 *New York Times*, 4 March 2005.

9 David Rieff, author of *A Bed for the Night: Humanitarianism in Crisis*, Simon & Schuster, New York, 2002.

10 Dag Hammarskjöld, UN Secretary-General 1953–61, *Der Spiegel*, 30 March 2005.

11 UNHCR figures, 2008.

Bibliography

Adelman, Howard. 'Why Refugee Warriors Are Threats'. *The Journal of Conflict Studies*, Vol. 18 (1998), no. 1 (Spring).

Baaijens, Arita. *Woestijnnomaden: trektocht door Sudan*. Amsterdam: Contact, 2003.

Clemens, Michael A., Steven Radelet and Rikhil Bhavnani. *Counting Chickens When They Hatch: The Short-term Effect of Aid on Growth*. Center for Global Development, working paper no. 44, 2004.

Cooley, Alexander and James Ron. 'The NGO Scramble: Organizational Insecurity and the Political Economy of Transnational Action'. *International Security*, Vol. 27 (2002), no. 1 (Summer), pp. 5–39.

Dallaire, Roméo. *Shake Hands with the Devil: The Failure of Humanity in Rwanda*. Canada: Random House, 2003.

Dam, Bette, *Expeditie Uruzgan – de weg van Hamid Karzai naar het paleis*. Amsterdam: De Arbeiderspers, 2009.

Dunant, Henri. *A Memory of Solferino*. ICRC, first edition 1863.

Easterly, William. *The Elusive Quest for Growth: Economists' Adventures and Misadventures in the Tropics*. Cambridge, Mass.: MIT Press, 2002.

Eggers, Dave. *What Is the What*. San Francisco: McSweeney's, 2006.

Frerks, G. and B. Klem. 'Tsunami Response in Sri Lanka: Report on a Field Visit from 6–20 February 2005'. Disaster Studies, Wageningen University and Conflict Research Unit, Clingendael Institute, March 2005.

Frerks, G., B. Klem, S. van Laar and M. van Klingeren. *Principles and Pragmatism: Civil–Military Action in Afghanistan and Liberia*. University of Utrecht and Cordaid, May 2006.

Glaser, Max. *Negotiated Access: Humanitarian Engagement with Armed Non-State Actors*. Carr Center for Human Rights Policy, Kennedy School of Government, Harvard University, May 2004.

Gutman, Roy, David Rieff and Anthony Dworkin (eds.). *Crimes of War*

2.0: What the Public Should Know. New York and London: Norton & Company, 2007.

Ignatieff, Michael. *The Warrior's Honor: Ethnic War and the Modern Conscience*. London: Penguin, 1998.

Jacques, Andy (ed.). *The Politics of Poverty: Aid in the New Cold War*. London: Christian Aid, 2004.

Kent, Randolph C. *Anatomy of Disaster Relief: The International Network in Action*. London: Pinter Publishers, 1987.

Klingeren, Marleen van. 'Communication in Conflict: NGO–Military Communication in Afghanistan and Liberia'. Nijmegen: Radboud University, Development Studies, 2007.

Lebanese Transparency Association/Tiri/UNDP. *Corruption in Post-Conflict Reconstruction: Breaking the Vicious Cycle*. 2005.

Lingsma, Tjitske. *Het verdriet van Ambon: een geschiedenis van de Molukken*. Amsterdam: Balans, 2008.

Maren, Michael. *The Road to Hell: The Ravaging Effects of Foreign Aid and International Charity*. New York: The Free Press, 1997.

Mills, Kurt and Richard J. Norton. 'Refugees and Security in the Great Lakes Region of Africa', *Civil Wars*, Vol. 5 (Spring, 2002), pp. 1–26.

Nijhuis, Minka. *Het huis van Khala: een familie in Bagdad*. Amsterdam: Balans, 2008.

Power, Samantha. *Chasing the Flame: Sergio Vieira de Mello and the Fight to Save the World*. New York: The Penguin Press, 2008.

Rieff, David. *A Bed for the Night: Humanitarianism in Crisis*. New York: Simon & Schuster, 2002.

Small, Hugh. *Florence Nightingale: Avenging Angel*. New York: St Martin's Press, 1998; reprinted 2000.

Stedman, Stephen J. and Fred Tanner (eds.). *Refugee Manipulation: War, Politics, and the Abuse of Human Suffering*. Washington: Brookings Institution Press, 2003.

Steering Committee of the Joint Evaluation of Emergency Assistance to Rwanda. *The International Response to Conflict and Genocide: Lessons from the Rwanda Experience*. London, May 1996.

Terry, Fiona. *Condemned to Repeat?: The Paradox of Humanitarian Action*. Ithaca: Cornell University Press, 2002.

Thompson, Allan (ed.). *The Media and the Rwanda Genocide,* with a statement by Kofi Annan. London: Pluto Press, 2007.

Veen, Roel van der. *Afrika: van de Koude Oorlog naar de 21e eeuw.* Amsterdam: KIT Publishers, 2004.

Waal, Alex de. *Famine Crimes: Politics and the Disaster Relief Industry in Africa.* London: African Rights and The International African Institute, 1997.

Watt, Patrick. *Millstone or Milestone?: What Rich Countries Must Do in Paris to Make Aid Work for Poor People.* ActionAid International UK and Brussels/Oxfam GB, Paris, March 2005.

Index